G000167748

*Critical Guides to French Texts*

EDITED BY ROGER LITTLE, WOLFGANG VAN EMDEN, DAVID WILLIAMS

DIDEROT

# Le Neveu de Rameau

J. F. Falvey

Senior Lecturer in French
University of Southampton

Grant & Cutler Ltd
1985

© Grant & Cutler Ltd
1985
ISBN 0 7293 0225 3

I.S.B.N. 84-599-0482-2

DEPÓSITO LEGAL: V. 425 - 1985

Printed in Spain by
Artes Gráficas Soler, S.A., Valencia
for
GRANT & CUTLER LTD
11 BUCKINGHAM STREET, LONDON W.C.2

# Contents

For Jane

## Prefatory Note

Two editions are referred to in the text: *Le Neveu de Rameau, Le Rêve de d'Alembert*, introductions, notes et annexes de Roland Desné et Jean Varloot, Editions Sociales, Coll. 'Essentiel', Paris 1984, and *Le Neveu de Rameau*, introduction, notes, chronologie, dossier et bibliographie par Jean-Claude Bonnet, Flammarion, Coll. 'GF', Paris 1983. These texts are referred to by page numbers only, the first reference being to Desné's edition, and the second, separated by an oblique stroke, to Bonnet's edition, thus: (p.75/45). Since my essay is intended to be of practical help to those studying the book for examination or similar purposes, I have bespattered it liberally with such references, from which the less harrassed non-specialist may well choose to avert his eyes. On the other hand, to avoid excessive annotation, I have been niggardly of references to my other sources (given in the form of italicised numbers, referring to the Select Bibliography at the end of this essay, followed where appropriate by the page reference), but none the less acutely conscious of my indebtedness for ideas, approaches, and insights, not only to published writings, but also to conversations with colleagues and with students. To all these sources, whose numbers far exceed those I have named in the references, I would like to record here my sincere thanks.

# 1. Introduction

## 1. The text and its mysteries

The text may be described as the account of a conversation between Diderot, an infinitely curious student of humanity, and Lui, Jean-François Rameau, nephew of the important French composer, Jean-Philippe Rameau, and himself a musician, but a strangely eccentric one, who has composed very little, and who sees himself as an unfulfilled genius. Diderot's characterisation of him seems to bear this out in the several directions taken by the dialogue, developments which suggest that Lui may well have genius, but of a sort which is doomed to remain unrecognised, because it exists in fields other than those prescribed by convention as appropriate for the display of exceptional gifts. These fields include sycophancy, for Lui prides himself on his professionalism in exploiting the vices of the rich by a variety of sharp practices ranging from flattery and minor deceptions, to crimes such as soliciting and procuring for immoral purposes. Diderot utilises this factor in order to conduct a satirical portrayal of the life styles and negative values of Lui's patrons and fellow parasites, and in particular, Palissot, who had attacked Diderot and those who had collaborated in his *Encyclopédie*.

Linked with Lui's assets as a social hanger-on is his talent for entertaining mime and accurate acting, a skill which he has carried to the highest level as a creative art-form, and which extends in an amazing way to become a miraculous manifestation of musical capabilities. A third field in which Luis displays an unorthodox form of potential genius is in his analysis of moral and social dynamics, where he presents a powerful case for individualism, amoralism, and anarchy, and for the possibility of genius in crime: 'le sublime dans le mal'. This descriptive account may appear straightforward enough: if so, it conceals a number of enigmas, some of them unlikely ever to be resolved.

Let us take first the question of Diderot's position in relation to the arguments advanced by Lui. A few critics consider that the enormity of Lui's amorality makes it perversè to think that Diderot could in any sense condone it: the conformist Moi must be the true Diderot, while Lui must be another person (presumably the real Jean-François Rameau) whose opinions he rejects (e.g. *4*, pp.20-24; *1*, pp.35-36, 42-43, but with reservations, pp.25-29). But this view is not universally accepted, for despite Diderot's exceptional clarity in certain respects, such as characterisation, description, and narration, it is noticeable that he ends the work without having given any decisive indication of his authorial preference for Moi's side of the argument, as opposed to Lui's side. It is true that the work is punctuated by passages of comment, incidental information and reflections, delivered in retrospect, that is to say, from a position different from that of the Moi of the dialogue. Desné's edition helpfully italicises these passages, which according to some commentators form a 'third voice' in addition to those of the Lui and Moi of the interchange. Some of these 'asides' seem to mark the ends of phases in the argument, thus affording guides to Diderot's sense of structure, but none of them provide any refutation from Diderot himself, of the logicality or possible truth of Lui's interpretation of society, morality or the human condition. The asides go no further than the expression of baffled surprise, that Lui is so gifted, logical, accurate and authoritative in his observations of behaviour and interpretation of motive (not least in respect of himself, for his non-hypocritical sincerity is repeatedly commended), and the expression of consternation, because Lui is at the same time so socially irresponsible and perverse, so horrifyingly and cynically amoral, so iconoclastic as regards conventions, decencies, altruism or respect for the rights of others.

In short, it is recognisable that Diderot has characterised not only the Moi of the dialogue but also the third voice, the 'author' of the asides, giving to both the values of a staid, middle class, responsible and respectable humanist. Suddenly confronted with the logic of nihilism and amoralism, Moi and the third voice (see pp.32-33/46-47, 96-97/62, 149/103-04) express an astonishment and bewilderment which could not have been felt by Diderot at the time of writing, since by then he would have been familiar with the view of society which he is in the process of explaining so comprehensively and confidently in the words of Lui. Moreover, Diderot the writer does not seem to share the horror of Moi: rather he seems to be amused at the power of Lui's vision to disturb the complacency of lay moralists (like himself), and in the closing pages deliberately paints the *philosophe*, likened to Diogenes, in drab and unsavoury colours, while Lui remains as sprightly and cogent as ever. We might thus speak of a fourth presence in this book, that of Diderot at the time of writing. But beyond the fact that he is presenting Lui's arguments in a spirit of amused mischief and self-criticism, he has carefully hidden any indication of the opinions of this authorial self.

This method of involving the reader by puzzling him seems already to have been grasped at least intuitively by a number of eighteenth-century novelists, e.g. Antoine Prévost, in *Manon Lescaut*, or Laclos, in *Les Liaisons dangereuses*. The author confronts his reader with the fascination of evil, or at any rate that which society currently considers to be evil, without guidance as to how we might resolve this paradox in human nature, or conduct ourselves in the face of it. We are simply left to ponder, or lament, or possibly feel liberated by, the convincingness of the psychology portrayed.

A second question posed by the text is that of its genre. There are so many loose ends that it is tempting to apply only terms with negative implications as the overall classification: terms like 'satire' (Diderot's own name for it), or 'sotie', or 'pot-pourri'. One critic, for example, has devoted a substantial book (*15*) to the style and manner of *Le Neveu de Rameau*, discovering delicate patterns and idiosyncratic structurings in Diderot's choice (whether by intention or by artistic intuition) of word, phrase and syntax, and perceiving his art as a kind of graceful verbal game-playing. Others have seen the book as a 'conversation', or an 'interview in the journalistic sense', and many, like Varloot (*16*, pp.16-17) and Roelens (*16*, p.30) have taken as the starting point for interpretation the dynamic of the dialogue form, in which the unresolved duality of two conflicting aspects of Diderot's thought and social attitudes produces the unity of the interchange itself, which generates at each moment new and exciting combinations and postures from the two contradictory sets of values, now considered as one because the movement, like that of two wrestlers, or of course two chess players, can occur only reciprocally. All these classifications and approaches imply — quite justifiably — open-endedness, inconclusiveness and impenetrability, and even if we attempt to classify the substance as opposed to the form, we still find ourselves drawn towards negative terms: nihilism, mystification, and (less frequently used, but still appropriate) irrationalism, anarchism or deconstructionism. However, it is more challenging and more satisfying to try to comprehend the characteristics of the work in an affirmative way, and this is probably best done by choosing to regard it as fiction, a short novel. It is admittedly a very unusual novel for its day, as it has little sequential story, and consists mainly of the dramatic encounter. At first sight it might appear to be disguised theatrical writing, but on closer acquaintance this proves not to be so. For the mimes are amusing, not so much in themselves, but through the brilliant prose in which Diderot describes them. Moreover their timing, while working well as narrative for reading, is less suitable for acting. Similarly the dialogue, while witty, pacy and exciting, is not always dramatic in the theatrical manner, but in a more intimate and reflective sense. For these and other reasons more readily sensed than analysed, stage adaptations of the piece (listed by Chouillet, 6, pp.255-56), while delightful to watch, unexpectedly fail to make more than passable theatre. Hence to appreciate the fineness of *Le Neveu de Rameau*, it is best to approach it as an early but masterly exploration of the potential of the encounter-conversation novel (e.g. Marguerite Duras's *Le Square*), where, in the course of a lengthy and digressive conversation, two personalities become closely known, two life-styles, orchestrated with sets of values, aspirations and frustrations, are called into complementary play, and brought convincingly and memorably to life.

A third set of questions is raised by the strange and ramified story of the manuscripts of the work, how they came — belatedly — to be found, released for publication, or in some cases lost again. A concise, well focused summary is given by Tancock (*7*, pp.19-24),[1] but research continues and in discussing Diderot's text, and the dates when he wrote it, we can speak only in provisional terms.

We do not know for sure that the encounter and argument between Lui and Diderot ever actually took place, but most critics accept that it did, and that it must have occurred in April 1761, when Dauvergne's opera *Hercule mourant*, which Lui is going to see at the end of the conversation, was running for its first nineteen performances. It could not have been much earlier, because Lui's wife did not die until January 1761 (pp.182-83/129-30), nor much later, because his son (first mentioned p.163/114) was to die in June 1761. It is therefore very probable that a version of the text, or part of it at least, was written in or shortly after April 1761. From that time onward Diderot kept the manuscript locked away as a closely guarded secret, though it is clear that he made numerous additions at various times, at least until 1774, and possibly until his death (in January 1784). One of several manuscript versions of it came into the hands of Goethe, who translated it into German and published it for the first time in 1805.

Such is the essence of the matter, but in 'the present state of the art' we do not know why Diderot (uncharacteristically) concealed from everyone, yet privately cherished, this remarkable manuscript, having several copies made, yet apparently making no provision for its publication, even after his death. It is, however, great fun to guess, and I shall be putting forward one possible conjecture later, in conclusion to the discussion of satirical elements.

A distinctive feature of *Le Neveu de Rameau*, one which probably arises from Diderot's intention never to publish it, is its readiness to name contemporaries. In discussing the work, explanations of a number of these allusions are essential for the

[1] The manuscript picked up by G. Monval in 1891 from a bouquiniste's box, and now in the Pierpont Morgan Library, New York, is considered the definitive version. All good editions have since been based on it (see Fabre, *3*, pp.xxii-xxvii).

understanding and the 'feel' of the text. Other allusions, e.g. the treatment of Mademoiselle Clairon, the significance of Bouret, or le Renégat d'Avignon (but see *17*) still await fully satisfactory explanations, and these little riddles are also part of the 'feel' of this text, where Diderot writes as if to an intimate friend, one who shared his interests and familiarity with contemporary personalities and news-items. I have not attempted to cover all the names alluded to in the text. Desné's concise and convenient footnotes, Fabre's richly informative endnotes, now supplemented by Chouillet's, and the less comprehensive but useful 'dossier' of extracts and digests provided by Bonnet, will enable the reader to extend his view of the contemporary background, which I have sketched only selectively.

Perhaps the most intriguing and tantalising of the problems is that raised by the quality of Diderot's prose style, manner and techniques. In one sense, Diderot is one of the most accessible of French writers, for it is possible, in any given passage, to pick out and explain the features and processes of his compelling wordings, and to show how closely they are matched to the internal logic of the substance. Yet commentary of this kind, if overdone, runs two risks. Sometimes it explains the writer's use of language so thoroughly that the spell is broken, or at least diminished, and no longer so readily experienced. Alternatively, it can leave the impression of speaking only of the obvious aspects of writerly quality, and of failing to capture or identify the living, magical elements of the artistry. The closeness with which Diderot's expression conforms with the particular ideas being presented adds further to the difficulty of making any meaningful global summing up of his art in generalised terms. With these things in mind, I have confined myself to giving stylistic commentaries on only a few passages, selected for their special relevance to the presentation of the meaning of the text, and I have deliberately left only scantily commented the splendid pages of the opening (pp.75-79/45-48). To the reader who wishes to understand Diderot's powers and qualities of penmanship, the best advice is that he turn, at the earliest opportunity, to the opening of *Le Neveu de Rameau*, and that he study closely, with repeated readings and careful reflection, the techniques of this exemplary introduction to the world of the novel, to the novelist (Diderot himself), and to the unforgettable character of Lui.

## 2. Interpretation and approach

When faced by problems of interpretation of an author's meaning, it is often helpful to look for signs of structuring, because the way in which he divides up, orders and presents the material must inevitably reflect something of his intentions (whether conscious or instinctive), of his focus, i.e. the relative importance he attaches to each part, and of the effect he wishes to make on his reader.

With *Le Neveu de Rameau*, however, we meet yet another enigma, for the structure has aptly been likened by several commentators (e.g. *2*, p.6) to a hanging mobile, an image which signifies that the major themes (genius, satire, music, education, and morality) do not come together in any fixed relationship, but co-exist in a changeable way, like the components in a mobile which, within controlled limits, swing and regroup themselves at different times, suggesting varying emphases and links. Thus, no two readers need necessarily interpret the meanings of the themes in the same way, nor need the same reader see the work in the same way on successive readings.

It follows that anyone studying this text is faced with the problem of where to start, and in which order to proceed, in dealing with its themes. My task would be more difficult if I were attempting to solve the riddle of Diderot's 'true' emphasis, or 'real' meaning. The present essay, however, has the slightly easier aim of presenting these problems to the reader, and of putting him in a position where he can confront them more directly for himself and, if he so wishes, venture his own conjectures. With this in view, it has seemed that the most effective way of conveying the mobile relationships of themes, is to present them, not in the sequence which Diderot has used, but commencing with the most clearcut and dramatically prominent part. This I take to be the discussion of music (pp.149-63/104-14; see also Goethe's comment, *2*, p.212), with its climactic mime sequence, its links with the title, and its lucidity arising from the fact that throughout the passage Moi is for once in agreement with Lui's views, making it clear that he regards him as an authority on the several aspects of music involved in the discussion.

A second readily perceived section is that in which Diderot satirises specific enemies (pp.120-48/80-103). The attack is arguably his initial motive for writing the book, and this function is easily discerned behind the transparent concealments, which were part of a well established tradition in satire. Thus we find Diderot introducing his main target, Palissot, only obliquely as part of Bertin's entourage, which itself appears at first to be mentioned only as the setting for the basic (and teasingly postponed) 'story' of *Le Neveu de Rameau*: the incident in which, despite his advanced skills as a sycophant, an ill-timed obscene joke, coupled with a momentary need for truth and personal dignity, causes Lui's irretrievable dismissal. But Diderot soon blurs our focus on this mishap, and we find ourselves retaining instead the hilarious — and often salacious — images of the grotesque hosts and their pretentious parasites, each stamped with a pettiness and disloyalty which disgusts Moi, particularly when Lui reveals a bedchamber secret. Another transparent concealment is noticeable when Diderot uses irony, seeming to exonerate the parasites (including Palissot) by asserting through Lui that the blame rests with the hosts, for their gullibility.

In its closing phases, the discussion moves from cheap parasitism to the theme of 'le sublime en mal' — excellence in criminality — in which Lui places himself fourth. The Renégat d'Avignon, and Diderot's prime target, Palissot, are equal seconds to the rich financier, Bouret, another piece of half-concealment and mystification.

Only slightly less clearcut is the discussion of genius (pp.79-100/48-65) which opens with a well-defined difference of opinion: Moi holds that men of genius advance the progress of culture and human achievement, while Lui asserts that the genius is, by his egoism and temperament, damaging and disruptive. From this point however the discussion slips into less easily perceived directions. Lui, apparently won over by Moi's argument, now expresses envy of the excellence, the creativity, and the self-fulfilment of the genius, manifested in contented sleep and window-shaking snoring; or (another shift) envy of the prosperity of the exceptionally accomplished sycophant. Each of these ambitions is illustrated with amusing mime, and there follows a passage of transition in which Lui further displays his gifts as a mimic-musician. His accompanying observations, to the effect that 'death is a great leveller', also adumbrate the speculation that genius, considered intrinsically as trans-cendental excellence, might exist not only in the recognised and socially accepted genres, but in other fields where it is not generally acknowledged, such as sycophancy and mimicry, and thus that Lui might be a genius. These are thematic questions which recur throughout the work and it is therefore appropriate to take the exploration and discussion of genius as the third main topic of this essay.

Having taken stock of the more readily identifiable sections, it is now time to look at those with less obvious shape and meaning, and we will examine next the final section of the book (pp.163-83/114-30). The central theme is the question of the power of society, and in particular of money, to subjugate and control the individual. The subsidiary theme of education in relation to morality emerges first: Lui claims that the effect of individual psychological make-up, inherited from parental characteristics ('la maudite molécule paternelle') is the over-riding factor in determining each person's career and morality. He argues the uselessness of all educational processes, except that of teaching the pupil how to attain riches and thus be able to fulfil his idiosyncratic vices, while avoiding disgrace or punishment.

The next subsidiary theme is the question of Lui's possible claim to genius. Why, asks Moi, has Lui not committed to paper his various talents, either as musician, critic, or inventor of para-sitic techniques? Lui describes his frantic but fruitless efforts to write, but concludes that Nature, through the 'molécule paternelle', has moulded him mis-shapen, as a practising parasite, but not as a man of letters. Again he brings the conversation back to money: poverty, hunger and the need to associate with depressing mediocrities like Palissot and other hangers-on, stifle any creative drives he might have had.

Sycophancy is the third and final subsidiary theme. Lui claims that each person is dependent, for the particular form of happiness and needs imposed on him by 'la molécule paternelle', on at least one other person, and must therefore humiliate himself, adopt cajoling postures, perform the fawning dances, wear the required masks. Moi agrees, affirming that even the king might not be exempt, for he must humour his mistress, but claims that the *philosophe*, who is indifferent to material gains or deprivations, is free from such indignities. Neither agrees with the other, so this question, like those of education, morality, and Lui's possible genius, is left hanging in the air: Is man fully dependent upon material things, and ethically determined by them, or can he be free by an assertion of mental and moral willpower?

We are now in a position to discern the structure and substance of that part of the book which is, on the surface, the least determinate in form and function (pp.100-19/65-79). The linked topics of education, money and morality can be discerned here, and the discussion is developed in similar fashion, both in substance and sequence, to the three themes recalled in the closing section of the book.

The opening discussion concerns the nature of knowledge, and of the processes of teaching and learning. Lui argues that 'ideal' teaching is impossible in the nature of things, but that the experienced teacher acquires 'tricks of the trade', involving deception and showmanship, but enabling him to give value for money in his lessons. The second subject pursues the theme of time and money in other branches of commerce: tricks of the trade (*idiotismes*) are harmless, so long as the immorality involved is not extended into other areas of the tradesman's life. In the final section, Lui passes in review the various concepts of non-religious morality entertained by Diderot and his associated *philosophes*: commercial ethics, *l'honneur*, stoical virtue, patriotism, friendship, duties to one's children, sexual morality, and finally the sentimental, tear-shedding morality of sensibility, so cherished by the eighteenth century, and not least by Diderot. Lui's comment is that each of these variants of self-restraint and altruism is 'vanité', the affectation of a prideful minority who, in their greed for a good image, are an embarrassment to their social contacts. Lui develops the point: self-indulgence, and pursuit of money, are more socially acceptable, because people can understand them, and because they form the only reliable supportive structures of societies and of human cohesion. Moi, totally shocked by this, is doubly confounded when Lui caps the section by speaking of his 'dignité', not in rational terms of lay morality or generalised social conscience, but as an irrational, inconsistent vitalistic impulse, peculiar to the individual and, like 'la molécule paternelle', irreducible to logical explanation or disciplined control (pp.119-20/80).

This important point is only counterbalanced in the closing section of the book by Moi's assertion — equally unreasoned — that it is possible for the intellectual (*le philosophe*) to retain his liberty, integrity and independence from the fawning dance of the world, to be 'un être dispensé de la pantomime' (p.180/127).

## 3. Structure

The foregoing outline interpretation should remove or reduce the obscurities of form and focus likely to be encountered at an initial reading of *Le Neveu de Rameau*, but it is now appropriate to restore the sections to the sequence in which Diderot has presented them, and to link the themes and ideas more securely to the text. This can most clearly and usefully be done in tabular form, as follows. References are given to the opening page of each component idea. Students of the text may find it helpful to refer back to this table from time to time while reading the following chapters.

75/45     *Introduction*: portrait of Lui 'au physique et au moral'.

79/48     *The nature of genius*: single-minded, ruthless, angular and possibly evil.

87/54     Lui's envy of geniuses, and his aspirations: mimes of:

independence and self-fulfilment.

a) Education and morality, for Lui's son, will inculcate worship of money, acceptance of self and needs, avoidance of disgrace, remorse and punishment.

169/119    b) Genius in conventional terms: why does Lui not write? He is prevented by 'la molécule' and by poverty.

176/124    c) The fawning dance of life. Lui: sycophancy is inseparable from the human condition. Moi opposes: the *philosophe* is free not to join the dance (180/127).

181/128    *Coda*: Money: Lui's last mime: his wife as source of income, recalling the tale of the Utrecht Jew (174/122) and the 'catins' of the Palais Royal gardens (75/45).

## 2. Music: Evolution or Revolution?

### 1. Les deux Rameau

Of Jean-François Rameau, the real-life original of the 'nephew' of Diderot's title, we have little factual information. The few certainties are as follows.

He was born in Dijon on 31 January 1716, and was still alive in 1766 when he was authorised to publish his autobiographical mock-heroic poem, *La Raméide*, a publication briefly reviewed by Grimm in his *Correspondance littéraire* of June-September 1766. He was married at Saint-Séverin, the parish church for a large area of the Left Bank, on 3 February 1757; in January 1761 his wife died, and in June 1761 his son died. The only other official mention of him is the police record of an incident in which he insulted the Directors of the Opéra in 1748. Fréron in 1757 describes, analyses and criticises in some detail J.-F. Rameau's *Nouvelles pièces de clavecin, distribuées en six suites* (see p.93/59). The music struck Fréron as descriptive in a rather blatant, but bold and novel way, and he found a few happy inventions and 'saillies musicales' to commend. The sixth suite consisted of three keyboard portraits of 'Les Trois Rameaux' (*sic*), the uncle Jean-Philippe, his father Claude, organist and harpsichordist at Dijon (Diderot's reference to him as an apothecary, pp.93/59, 175/124, is another little mystery), and Jean-François himself.

A more substantial picture can be conjured up around these skeletal facts if we accept as true the five contemporary accounts of Jean-François. All five are conveniently assembled by Fabre (*3*, pp.243-54) and four by Bonnet (*2*, pp.203-11). From a remark by Cazotte it is deducible that the probable earliest date for Jean-François's death is 1770. The accounts are in general agreement upon the major features conveyed in Diderot's novel. Fréron (in 1757), Piron (in 1764) and Cazotte (published in 1816) testify to his humour, originality, lovable eccentricity, great and varied gifts, especially for music, his many different facets and unpredictableness. Cazotte claims to have written *La Nouvelle Raméide* (favourably reviewed by Grimm, who had dismissed *La Raméide* as a rigmarole of rubbish) as a joke played on Jean-François, who was a lifelong friend, and who had not objected. It is in this work that we find the thesis about the value of the (long defunct) office of jester to the king, and the eminent suitability of J.-F. Rameau for the post, should it be re-established (see pp.133-34/91). Cazotte speaks of his upright nature and his burning ambition both as musician and as man of letters. Both Cazotte and Grimm tell us that he could be sometimes very amusing, perceptive and rich in good ideas, but sometimes wrong-headed and irritating.

Grimm is the only hostile commentator, and the only one to denigrate his intelligence, speaking of his 'imagination bête et dépourvue d'esprit'. From Grimm comes the claim that Jean-François had personally told him that he studied Molière, giving the same reasons as Lui (pp.132-33): 'J'y apprends ce qu'il ne faut pas dire mais ce qu'il faut faire'. Mercier (in 1788) says little about his character, but reports his theory that all human motivation, even the most exalted behaviour or creativity, could be attributed to the need to eat, 'la mastication'. We can readily link this to Lui's views on the centrality of money in human affairs (pp.166/116, 170-71/120). Mercier also tells of Jean-François's father, whose wildness as a young man, and resourceful ingenuity as showman, entertainer and moneymaker, seem to match Lui's characteristic (e.g. pp.174-75/123-24).

Unlike that of his scapegrace nephew, Jean-Philippe Rameau's life-story is one of success and international acclaim. His genius rapidly brought him fame and earned him a significant place in the history of music, so information about him is easily found in many studies and in standard works of reference. It will however be convenient for the understanding of *Le Neveu de Rameau* to summarise his career and to indicate the substance of some of Diderot's allusions to him.

J.-P. Rameau was born at Dijon in 1683, the son of an organist in the cathedral, and began his career as organist and harpsichord teacher in several French provincial towns. He settled in Paris in the late 1720s, his arrival there being preceded by the renown of his book on the theory of sound vibrations, musical acoustics and the generation of chords, *Traité de l'harmonie réduite à son principe* (1722), later amplified and republished in 1750 as *Démonstration du principe de l'harmonie, servant de base à tout l'art musical*, a work in which, according to a none-too-reliable contemporary, he was helped by Diderot. D'Alembert, Diderot's main assistant in the production of the *Encyclopédie*, wrote a vulgarisation of Rameau's book, clarifying the obscure mathematical theorising, under the title *Eléments de musique et théorique pratique, suivant les théories de M. Rameau* (1752). By the middle 1750s, however, Rameau's theories had lost favour with the *encyclopédistes*, being superseded by the mathematically clear and experimentally well-founded explanations of cord-vibration being put forward by Daniel Bernouilli. Lui's remark (pp.80-81/ 49) 'pourvu que les cloches ... continuent de résonner la douzième et la dix-septième tout sera bien' reflects this clash of theories, as Fabre explains (*3*, pp.125-26).

Rameau enjoyed a virtually unchallenged eminence in Paris, rapidly achieving and then consolidating his European fame as the main creator of a distinctively French form of opera. In this he was continuing the tradition begun by Jean-Baptiste Lulli, 1632-87 (pp.152/106, 159/111, 162/113), known as 'le Florentin', who had commenced the process of adapting the opera forms of his native Italy to Parisian taste, under the influence of the classical French theatre and especially that of Molière. André Campra, 1660-1744, and Jean-Joseph Mouret, 1682-1738 (p.152/106) were intermediary figures who heralded the work of Rameau but who were eclipsed by him. Rameau's major opera-ballets included *Les Indes galantes*, 1735 (pp.88/ 55, 152/106, 162/114), *Castor et Pollux*, 1735, his masterpiece, and *Les Fêtes d'Hébé ou les Talents lyriques*, 1739 (p.152/106). Apart from their musical beauty his works were admired for a new richness and dramatic vitality in the orchestration, and for their recitative — linking passages between arias, halfway between speech and singing — in which he had introduced a new formality, criticised by some as being too geometric, but adding elegance and diversity to the available chords for the 'basse fondamentale' (pp.100/65, 110/72), the harpsichord accompaniment.

Jean-Philippe's operas were still attracting audiences at the time of his death in 1764, and he himself was the recipient of many honours, including a pension from the Directors of the Opéra, ennoblement and the position of composer of the royal chamber music, and finally a public funeral. His last ten years were however embittered by anxiety over competition from the Italian *opéra bouffe*. Diderot seems to have sensed in this conflictual situation a symbol of untutored, natural inspiration, or genius, disrupting an entrenched but sterile conventionalism in art forms, and perhaps, more broadly, of anarchic vigour challenging the fossilised social establishment.

It is therefore worth while to look closely at the clash of operatic cultures known as the *Guerre des bouffons*. A performance by the Paris Opéra in 1752 of *Omphale* (1701, music by André-Cardinal Destouches, 1672-1749) drew from Melchior Grimm, the German critic with whom Diderot was for a long time closely associated in the *Correspondance littéraire*, an essay entitled *Lettre sur 'Omphale'*. While not directly critical of Rameau, the letter challenged the authenticity of French opera, with its many national characteristics, including use of the French language, and touched off an intense pamphlet battle between its supporters, associated with the Académie Royale de Musique, and the supporters of Italian opera, that is to say, works written and sung in Italian by Italians, accepted as the true form of opera throughout Europe, except in France. As a result of the heated discussions, a group of Italian singers was invited to perform at the Paris Opéra. Their major success with Pergolese's *La Serva Padrona* in August 1752 created a divisive cultural sensation, and provided a talking point for critics and experts on both sides in the argument of 'taste'. Was the Italian music, with its amusements and lack of inhibitions, a betrayal of national standards and academic values, a capitulation to vulgarity and mere sensationalism? Or was it a rich new field of authentic naturalism, of vigorous primal inspiration, capable of liberating and re-vitalising a derivative and worn-out Parisian musical tradition, too theoretical, too academic, too dependent on accepted rules, forms and embellishments?

Lui's reply to Moi (pp.152-54/106-07), agreeing that French music is 'un peu plate' can be understood in this context, as can his ironic demand for the suppression of the beautiful *Stabat Mater* by Giovanni Pergolese, 1710-36, the tragically short-lived composer of *La Serva Padrona*, sung with such devastating success by the visiting 'maudits bouffons'. 'Bouffon' here does not of course mean 'buffoon', but one who sings in the Italian *opéra bouffe*, a short light opera, humorous but not necessarily farcical. By the eighteenth century, *intermezzo* or *intermède* had come to mean the same as *opéra bouffe*, a light entertainment often put on between the acts of serious operas or plays. *La Serva Padrona* was a two-act intermezzo, and the Italian phrases sung so enthusiastically by Lui ('Aspettare...' etc., p.156/109) are the opening lines of its three main arias, showing beyond doubt that he was being ironic in calling the *bouffons* 'accursed'. The continuing popularity of Italian operas posed a threat to the more refined Opéra Français, whose house, directed by Rebel and Francœur, was in the Impasse d'Orry, a cul-de-sac near the Palais Royal. As the management fought to retain audiences, Rameau became a key figure in the *querelle des bouffons*, for his great, and therefore reliably popular, operas of the 1730s were performed with increased frequency, as was his opera-ballet, *Platée ou Junon jalouse*, (1749), a witty and highly competent parody of the new Italian style and forms which enjoyed considerable success.

In this position, Rameau became even more widely known, through the pamphleteering efforts of foes as well as friends, and his arrogance, crustiness, ill-natured and absent-minded aloofness to his wife and family (e.g. pp.80-81/49, 83-84/51, 93-94/59) offered rich pickings to the gossip journalists of the period. And while all this was going on, not only were his theories of sound-vibrations being superseded, but many of his musical ideas, e.g. those on recitative and 'déclamation', were coming under the clever and persuasive criticism of Jean-Jacques Rousseau who was contributing articles on music to

Diderot's *Encyclopédie*, items later collectively published as *Dictionnaire de musique*. In 1753 appeared Rousseau's *Lettre sur la musique française* in which Italian music was commended for qualities considered to be lacking in French composers and in the currently accepted academic rules. Despite these odds, Rameau remained a doughty and formidable fighter, and the performances of his works continued to keep a sizeable sector of the opera-going public, and the music critics, faithful to French traditions. By his personal nature, professional standing, and tenacious resistance to the oncoming new wave, he provided Diderot with a prominent archetypal figure, emblematic of the old order and solid, tried and proven achievements and standards, a Pantaloon-like symbol in some ways, against which 'le neveu' could be drawn as Harlequin, the mercurial, undisciplined, but inspirational proponent of intuition, inventiveness, spontaneous exuberance and of as yet untried values and paths. The conjunction of 'les deux Rameau' in the title of the book aptly catches this dichotomy, which subtends not only the discussion of music, but in its social sense, the whole of the dialogue.

## 2. Lui's ideas: the grass roots of song

Lui's ideas on music fall into place in this context: they are expressed dramatically and forcefully, and give a fair impression of the 'pro-*bouffon*' side of the *querelle* — warts and all, as we shall quickly see.

*Truth to nature.* Lui's ideas on the nature of music revolve around the principle of imitation, and of fidelity to nature, summed up in his demand for 'le vrai...qui engendre le bon... d'où procède le beau' (pp.154-55/108). The artist must seek to discern, represent and convey the basic realities ('la nature') of humanity and of the environment, and to avoid any artifices, in manner or in the creative process, which might lead him 'trop loin de la simple nature' (pp.160-61/112). If his imitation of authentic natural forms is faithful, 'le bon' and 'le beau' will, it seems, take care of themselves, and Lui's remarks are noticeably lacking in anything explicit about quality, whether in the moral or the artistic sense. This is one of several shortcomings in his account of musical aesthetics.

*Energy*. Although critics sometimes refer to Lui's ideas as 'naturalism' or 'verism', they have only a little in common with late nineteenth-century Naturalism in French literature, or the 'verismo' in Italian opera which followed from it. Rather than suggesting a slice of everyday life, the artist must select subjects which represent energy: 'n'allez pas croire que le jeu des acteurs de théâtre et leurs déclamations puissent nous servir de modèles ...Il nous le faut énergique, moins maniéré, plus vrai' (p.161/112). This means that, where the subject is human, the artist must seek moments of visible, if not intense, emotion: '... une passion, n'importe laquelle, pourvu que par son énergie elle méritât de servir de modèle au musicien' (p.162/113). He does not, however, say anything here of the creative energy of the composer, or suggest ways in which the genius differs from the musician of mere talent and competence. It is nevertheless within these two general terms of reference — truth to nature, and energy or passion — that he explains the specific art of the opera composer, and his criteria for evaluating such pro-ductions.

*Song and melody*. 'What is *un chant*?' asks Lui. The word can mean either 'song', that is, words and music, or melody only, and in answering, Lui mingles the two meanings, causing some slight but not crucial obscurity. He defines *un chant* (pp.149-51/104-05) as imitation in sounds, on a conventionally agreed scale, either by voice or instrument, of 'des bruits physiques' or of the accents of human emotion ('la passion'). The composer's model in nature for *le chant* is 'la déclamation', and here a real obscurity arises, because 'declamation' in French as in English has a wide range of meaning. Let us however for the moment take it in its broadest sense of any form of articulate utterance. Reduced to this level, the quality of song-melody is represented and judged by Lui in simplistic terms: he likens *déclamation* (utterance) and *chant* (melody) to two lines which we today may readily think of as lines on a graph representing rise and fall of tone on the vertical scale, against lapse of time, hence speech rhythm, on the horizontal axis. The more frequent the points of coincidence between the lines, that of the model, natural speech ('déclamation forte et vraie') and the line of the composed melody, the more the 'chant' (now meaning 'words and music') will be authentic and hence, in Lui's terms, beautiful: '...plus le chant sera vrai et plus il sera beau'.

*Declamation.* To return to the question of the meaning of this word, we can note that in the foregoing discussion Lui has been using it in the less frequent sense of 'delivery of an impassioned rather than a reasoned speech'. He goes on to cite examples (pp.150-51/105-06) of operatic arias where the composer has closely reflected the rhythm and the rise and fall of speech, in setting to music lines which strike today's reader as blatantly theatrical (e.g. 'O terre, reçois mon trésor'), and he commends the richness of this approach, which opens up 'une variété infinie' of characteristic ways in which emotion inflects voice-tones (compare also pp.161-62/113). Catching the rhythms of speech offers a still wider palette: the would-be composer has only, it seems, to be 'un habile homme', and to listen to accent patterns in normal speech, to have both melodic line and rhythm suggested to him: 'Accent is the seedbed of melody', he claims, citing a Latin tag from Martianus Capella's *Satyricon*.

*French and Italian as languages for opera.* At a later stage, Lui's meaning for 'déclamation' changes, and he expressly demands that the composer's model should *not* be 'déclamation', using the word now in its more frequent sense of 'delivery of an utterance in a theatrical or rhetorical way' (see above, under '*Energy*'). The proper model should be the uninhibited outbursts of real-life speakers: 'C'est au cri animal de la passion à nous dicter la ligne qui nous convient', i.e. 'le cri animal ou de l'homme passionné' (pp.159-61/111-12). We must recognise however that by this stage Lui is pointing out and deploring the artificiality of the writing of French playwrights and librettists (*les poètes lyriques*) as opposed to their Italian counterparts who are more natural in their wording and phrasing of 'déclamations' and in setting these words to music, and far ahead of Jean-Philippe Rameau, once regarded (in the

1730s) as the master of 'la déclamation musicale'. Lui points out
two disadvantages for the French opera composer: one is in the
French language itself, which is stilted, resistant to inversion,
and unsuitable to the relaxed naturalness of Italian; the other is
in the highly stylised tradition of French classical literature, full
of 'sentences ingénieuses, des madrigaux...délicats'. He lists in
contrast the many passionate qualities of lyrics by Italian
writers, who would never contemplate any such formal
elegances as 'esprit...épigrammes...jolies pensées'.

All of these ideas go some way towards explaining the wide-
spread and increasing success of the Italian opera, with its
popular appeal and its more natural, spirited and emotive
effects, and indeed the ideas reflect and catch the spirit of those
to be found in the hastily written pamphlets of the *Guerre des
bouffons* of the 1750s. They do not, however, tell us anything
about the quality of musical artistry, or about the magic by
which a musical genius can carry us, through his creations, into
another more orderly, serene and satisfying world. Fabre
mentions this thinness of ideas, and suggests that Diderot was
not deeply interested in, or particularly well informed on,
musical matters. He points out in his notes numerous slight mis-
quotations in the extracts sung by Lui; he explains that Lui's
extravagant admiration for Egidio Duni, the Italian expatriate
composer of Parisian successes in the field of *opéra bouffe*, was
misplaced, because within a year after the supposed date of the
conversation (1761), Duni disappeared from prominence after
the failure of his *La Plaideuse*.

Fabre's conclusion, that Diderot never bothered to revise or
update this section on music is strongly supported by the fact
that Lui mentions, as up-and-coming opera writers, only the
relatively minor figures working in the 1750s, such as D.M.B.
Terradellas, 1711-51, T. Traetta, 1729-79 and P.B. Trapasi
(known as Metastase) 1698-1772 (pp.159-60/111, and see also
Fabre's notes, *3*, pp.225-26), but omits mention of the more
colourful and sensational impact on the Parisian musical world
of the late 1760s and the 1770s made by major visitors such as
Mozart, Gluck and Niccolo Piccini. Fabre's further conclusion,

that these numerous inadequacies in the section on music account for the relative lack of attention which it has attracted from critics, is certainly persuasive, and his comment that the section is of minor value, because it is one of the 'zones anciennes' of the book, 'conservés telles quelles, d'où la vie s'est retirée', has generally passed unchallenged.

An alternative evaluation is, however, also tenable. It is true that the ideas are not as ample or accurate as they might be, but they are, by that very token, more immediately intelligible, more graspable, exciting and provoking of reaction from the reader, perhaps even more so because Moi does not contest them. They are also well in keeping with Lui's character: gifted, but hasty, impulsive, and mentally agile rather than consistent; and they catch very vividly the atmosphere of the *Guerre*, a lively and healthy moment in cultural history, when people were taking sides, many of them looking with disrespect at the Académie de Musique and at its protégé, the Opéra Français, and getting involved in an amateurish, non-pedantic way, with music, not only in terms of theories, but mainly as a performing art, with its entertainment personalities and its popular favourites.

## 3. Lui's mime and Diderot's manner

It seems barely possible, to judge by the tone of the passage on music, and that of the references to the matter elsewhere in the book, that the shortcomings in Lui's ideas on music ('idées banales et courtes', says Fabre) are intentional on Diderot's part. But is *is* possible to argue that, whether by deliberate design, lucky accident, or sub-conscious artistic intuition, they accord felicitously with the rest of the section on music, and make it the most attractive one in the book. It is in the first place easy to contest Fabre's view that, because this section, written in 1761, was never subsequently revised, 'the life has gone out of it'. The opposite could well be affirmed: by virtue of being written down all of a piece, probably shortly after a real encounter and conversation, this section has kept its immediacy, animation and spontaneity; re-working, and especially didactic up-dating, could easily have spoiled this precious quality. In any case one can hardly consider lifeless a section which contains the most flamboyant and exuberant passage of the book, perhaps even in Diderot's writings as a whole: the sustained mime in which Lui impersonates orchestra, opera and ballet almost, or so Diderot suggests, all at once (pp.156/108 'Et puis le voilà...' to 159/111 '...il faudra bien qu'ils viennent.').

But what is still more intriguing is the fact that many of the shortcomings noted above in the ideas (lack of explanation of concepts: *le bon*, *le beau*, as qualities; *le vrai*, *la vérité*; energy in the sense of creative artistry and invention, of passionate, uninhibited and convincing utterance; the transporting magic of genius, the compelling originality and authority of statement ) — all these gaps are made good through images rather than arguments, by Lui's mime and its miraculous effects on Moi and the bystanders. There is some suggestion that Diderot was doing this consciously: 'l'homme, comme l'enfant, aime mieux s'amuser que s'instruire', says Moi, of Lui's performance (p.161/112).

Rather, however, than embark on any special pleading for this alternative reading and evaluation, or on any speculation as to how far Diderot planned this effect, I shall end this chapter with a close commentary on Diderot's craftsmanship in handling the mime-sequence. The focal point of the passage is Lui's ability to comprehend and interpret music, through mime so all-embracing and accurate that it almost defies belief. Diderot's task is to induce us to believe, and to impart to us the excitement and pathos of Lui's performance. The passage represents the climax of the book, both dramatically and intellectually, for after it we can no longer dismiss Lui as an inconsequential clown: his gifts, and claim to genius of a strange sort, are shown to be valid. So Diderot is on his mettle, and it is fascinating to see how he employs his writerly skills, and to guage his success in meeting the challenge. As is often the case with eighteenth-century writing, the structure, both overall and in detail, has been logically thought out; this passage falls readily into five sections, which it is instructive to identify and analyse.

(1) The first section, 'Et puis le voilà...' to 'du caractère de

l'air', is separated into two areas of visual and auditory imagery, by Lui's hit-or-miss quotations from arias.

(a) In the first (to '...qui se prépare') Diderot stresses (i) that Lui's performance is starting up (*se met à, commençait à*) and gathering momentum (*vinrent ensuite, scène nouvelle qui se prépare*); and (ii) that his physical behaviour is becoming increasingly deranged: movement and gesture become more violent (*se promener, levant les mains et les yeux, gestes, grimaces, contorsions*); singing becomes louder, more articulate (*murmurant, chanter tout bas, élevait le ton*). (iii) A third component is formed by comments from Lui (*si cela est beau*, underlining his sensitivity, and linking with the previously adumbrated concepts, *le beau, le bon* etc.), and from Moi, psychological interpretations of the physical behaviour (*entrer en passion, se passionnait davantage, voilà la tête qui se perd*). Moi's aside here sums up this opening crescendo of agitation, and launches us into the following phase: 'en effet il part...'. The lively inflections of wording in the comments of both remind us that, in addition to any other interests, we should remain aware of the joyous, even hilarious aspects of this performance.

One feature of Diderot's manner already noticeable is the way in which each of these component effects (starting up, physical movements, comments) is not grouped together in a block, but strung out in a series of near-synonyms, or of similar observations, as listed above, each string intertwining with the others. The effect is to convey movement, plenitude and variety of image, while retaining clarity, because each component thread of imagery is reinforced by repetition of its central idea, through recurrent synonyms. One might criticise the technique as crude, but it can hardly be denied that it is lively and powerful.

In the second area, (b), 'Il entassait...' to '...de l'air'), the intertwining thread technique is less conspicuous, and instead Diderot uses additional wording devices to amplify the general idea, which is that of massive accumulation and violent diversity of references and snatches from operas, building up to a first climax of almost chaotic richness. The effect of multiplicity, for example, is underlined by blocks of associated adjectives (*airs italiens*, *français*, *tragiques* etc., *furieux*, *radouci* etc.), or nouns (*démarche*, *maintien* etc.); by constructions involving distributive adverbs (*tantôt...tantôt...*; *Ici...là...*; *successivement...jamais...*), and by contrasts (*enfers...haut des airs...*). Particularly visible is Diderot's handling of rhythmic pulses, through simple sentence components and repetition: *il est prêtre, il est roi...*; *il menace, il commande...*; followed by a series of phrases all beginning 'il' which quicken the pace: *il se désole, il se plaint, il rit*. And a solid, rhythmically satisfying sentence rounds off this first climax as Diderot emphasises the musical sensitivity and dramatic convincingness of Lui.

(2) A second climax is presented in the next section, 'Tous les pousse-bois...' to '...et les dénaturait'. Diderot diversifies the form by portraying more clearly the onlookers and — very important for the sense of the passage and indeed of the book — the reality of the effect upon them.

(a) The opening part, to '...Petites Maisons', gives an expanding view, moving outward from Lui and Moi, with a suggestion of concentric circles: immediately around them, the awe-struck chess-players, then outside the café, passers-by, crowding round for a glimpse in through the windows, of the entertainment; then Moi, with a sense of Paris as a whole, thinks of the cab-journey which would be necessary if Lui, as seems likely, were to lose his wits entirely, and had to be bundled off to the madhouse (Petites Maisons) at Saint Germain des Prés.

(b) In the next part (to '...éprouvée') Diderot again uses intertwining strings of component images. (i) There is Lui's mastery of music and theatre, and his infallible sense of selection (*le plus beaux endroits; endroits où le musicien s'est montré comme un grand maître*), his understanding of the composer's intentions, and his respectful interpretation of them (*précision*, *vérité*, *chaleur*, *délicatesse*, *force*, *douleur*). (ii) There is also his remarkable agility in flitting from one instrument or voice to another in order to present the essential parts, and his barely credible achievement in retaining the unity of the total effect (*Tout y était..., les liaisons et l'unité de tout*). (iii) And with it all Diderot stresses the genuineness of the moving effect on the onlookers (*qui en [des larmes] arrachèrent à tous les yeux; s'emparant de nos âmes*). The import of these three component themes is that Lui is truly gifted, and to a superlative degree (*situation la plus singulière*).

(c) An aside from Moi outlines the strangely contradictory emotions he feels: unfeigned admiration, also compassion, for these real gifts, subjected to the indignity of non-achievement; yet there is at the same time a sense of the absurd, the grotesque (*les dénaturait*). This element led Otis Fellows (*12*, pp.194-96) to think that Diderot did *not* consider Lui to be a true genius, but from the context (i.e., from (b) above) it seems probable that Diderot is indicating a kind of pathos, and a feature of extreme originality: since Lui is performing in an unaccepted medium, and one of the most ephemeral, his immense output in terms of artistic resource and ingenuity, and lifelong dedication to the beauty of music, is incongruous, out of proportion to the ends achieved, and to the small respect his creative energy-surge commands.

(3) The third and major climax occurs in the section 'Mais vous seriez...' to '...tout à fait perdue'.

(a) Diderot begins by evoking the joyous gusto of musical creation, through the comic impact of the ingenious impressionist in imitating the sounds of five different instruments. This image of intricate complexity and rapid, skilful movements becomes even more complex, inflated and exceptional with the lists of various groups which Lui represents: dancers, singers, male and female, and the whole orchestra, until he is darting from part to part like a thing possessed (*énergumène*).

(b) A realistic detail, briefly interposed, conveys the intensity of this climactic point: the heat of the crowded café is stifling, and we are given a close-up view of the way Lui's perspiration affects his face-wrinkles, wig-powder and coat-collar, a detail chosen to symbolise frenzied exertion.

(c) At the grand climax of the performance Diderot strives to suggest the majesty, poetry and enchantment which Lui's 'music' conjures up, using images of intense emotions and of the splendours of nature. Once again, repetitions of simple sentence structures build up forceful rhythms, excitement, and finally produce a calm, beautifully controlled rounding off: 'Il pleurait, il..., il..., il...; c'était une femme...c'était...; un temple qui..., des oiseaux qui..., des eaux qui...' etc. A flurry of words, itemising the effects of a storm, forms a climax, and then, to bring the passage to a serene close: 'c'était la nuit...c'était l'ombre et le silence...'.

(4) The essence of the next section is to show that Lui, following the visionary excursion into the realm of music, is 'Epuisé de fatigue', and awaiting 'le retour de ses forces'. Diderot's efforts to elaborate round this simple idea are interesting examples of pre-romanticism, but to today's taste at least, suffer from rather forced sentimentalism and pointless melodrama, as Lui awakes, unable to remember where he is.

(5) In the closing section, 'Ensuite il ajouta...' to '...qu'ils y viennent', Diderot re-finds his control of manner. He exploits the impact of this spectacular mime sequence, symbol of revolutionary, elemental power and inspiration, tailoring the image neatly back into the discussion. Lui looks at the future of French opera, pays limited tributes to what was good in the past school of Lulli, Campra and Rameau, and observes in his racy style that even good things come to an end (*les Rois sont passés*), that culture, like everything else, evolves. He again flops exhausted on his bench, and has to be refreshed with copious supplies of beer and lemonade, which prove instantaneously efficacious and fuel further conversational flights about 'l'énergie' and 'la passion'.

In relation to the major currents in the development of Western European writing an interesting feature of the substance and form of this passage is the combination of elements relating to two recognisable concepts of literature. On the one hand there is Diderot's sense of formal overall structure, producing the logical framework of sections, and the oratorical stylistic effects, colourless in themselves, because they rely on commonplace and functional parts of speech (e.g. *tantôt*, *c'était*, repetitions of 'il' etc.), but interesting in the rhythms and other supportive effects which Diderot can generate through them. Such skills, common to Montesquieu, Voltaire and others, relate to Classicism, and to the tradition of formal elegance, summed up in the precept, commonplace from the mid-seventeenth century onwards, 'plaire et instruire' echoed here in evolved form by Diderot (p.161/112). On the other hand, we find him attempting approaches later to become associated with Romanticism: the prose-poem, or purple passage, of which this is an example (compare the image of the tree, p.86/53), the view of the hero as misfit and outcast, isolated from the herd by his exceptional gifts, and grasp of deep spiritual realities, but courageous in his originality and steadfast in his revolt and protest; the sardonic half-mocking humour with which the hero is presented by the author; the portrayal of intense, overcharged emotion; the supple use of language, and of non-noble words and forms; the reference to nature as true, authentic, and opposed to convention (even perhaps to civilisation), which is seen as tawdry and meaningless.

Such, then, is Diderot's handling of the climactic passage of his book. How far he has succeeded in meeting this challenge, and in his artistry as a writer, is a question which must now be left to each individual to ponder and to judge for himself.

### 3. Satire: Parasites, Criminals and Enemies of the Encyclopédie

By far the most humorous part of *Le Neveu de Rameau* is the section containing Diderot's satirical attacks. In portraying his targets, whether individuals or groups, he calls into play his rich gifts for creating lively and convincing human beings, and in dwelling on their unsavouriness as people, he displays his even richer talents for malicious, and especially for bawdy, comicality. It is understandable that a satirical work should carry only brief information about the positions held by those attacked, or about the ways in which they had offended the author. Such terseness not only speeded the pace of the writing, but also added piquancy in that it gave the writer's contemporaries an amusing chance to utilise and show off their knowledge of fashionable society gossip and scandals. That kind of appeal is of course very transient: within a decade or so the necessary background knowledge is no longer common. But as time passes the allusions can acquire a different appeal, and Diderot's book is a case in point.

By inducing us to laugh at the antics of the targets, he has, by the same token, compelled us to envisage them, to accept tacitly their existence, for in order to enjoy the jokes, we have to visualise the people and situations, at least in outline and caricatural form. With our interest thus captured, our curiosity is awakened, and we find ourselves wanting to know about the real misdeeds and follies which Diderot leaves half-hidden behind his allusions. Such at least is one explanation of the way in which satire and humour work on the reader's mind and produce the effect of immortalising the victims in all the ugliness and absurdity which their attacker wishes to heap on them. Let us apply the theory to the text and see how the social panorama behind Lui and Moi opens out.

## 1. Humour and impact

We will begin by examining the two high points of Diderot's humour, that is to say, low points of his bawdiness, for both jokes are obscenely indecent. The first is of major importance to the 'plot', such as it is, since it is the long deferred tale of how Lui, the all but flawless hanger-on, came to be jettisoned (pp.135-36/92-93). As usual in the best of Diderot's writing, the narration is structured with a nice sense of form, and since in this instance it is the telling of a joke, it is also unfolded with an impeccable sense of raconteur's timing. The 'punch-line' is preceded by what seems to be a set of irrelevancies: we meet the seedy editor of one of the five gossip journals, a list by which Diderot neatly ensures that his readers know some of the sources from which he drew the fashionable scandals he alludes to; we are told of the parasites crawling out of their nests at meal time, a joke already well worked in *La Nouvelle Raméide*; there is a reference to their down at heel elegance: if you arrive with your only suit of clothes muddied, you must hope to talk the hard-headed Savoyard clothes- and boot- brusher, selling his services outside the host's front door, into giving you yet another quick clean-up, on the promise of a tip at some future date.

The realism of these details, and the facility with which Diderot produces them, suggest that he had personal experience of the situation. But we should also notice the choice of image, for beneath the apparent irrelevance, the details set the scene exactly for the crucial error made by Lui in a precarious situation. Just such another closely observed detail of custom, aptly selected to prepare for the punch-line, is Lui's account of the progressive 'descent' of each new cultural lion, from the head of the dinner-table on his first appearance, to the bottom. It comically epitomises one of the unspoken conditions of the parasite's existence, which becomes increasingly threatened as the host's tolerance of him wears thinner. It causes merriment among the hangers-on, including Mademoiselle Hus, who all know that they are totally dependent on their entertainment value. But Lui's brash remark referring to this dependency causes irreparable annoyance to the host, Bertin, because it is too near the knuckle, 'une vérité amère' (p.128/87, compare pp.91/57-58, 'la raison', 'le sens commun').

The breath-taking vulgarity of the punch-line itself is an essential part of the effect of unthinking outspoken tactlessness. It has in its day caused commentators and translators not otherwise noted for an excess of coyness, to leave it in Diderot's racy Italian (e.g. Fabre, *3*, p. 207, Tancock, *7*, p.85). However such squeamishness is misplaced here: to understand the effect we must understand the tones: '...beside me, sitting here, as I always do, like a majestic prick between two pillocks'.

So too in the second joke vulgarity is an essential part of the shock-effect. Moi is scandalised at Lui's unkind revelation of how the peace of the night was shattered by a hullabaloo which brought the whole household running to the master's bedchamber, where they found that Miss Hus, driven frantic by sexual arousal, had gained the upper hand and was trying to extract satisfaction by bouncing energetically upon the none-too-majestic Bertin. This time the punch-line is in French, and deliberately catches a crude earthiness of tone as Lui evokes a massive anvil descending upon a tiny hammer (p.144/99).

One purpose of these jokes is obviously to titillate and to amuse, but other important functions are to create the effects of firstly, a sordid, animal-like level of behaviour, the disgusting activities of depraved degenerates, and secondly a caricatural, grotesque impact. In this latter, Diderot aptly indicates the similarity between the manner he is aiming at, and that of France's greatest fiction humorist, Scarron, creator of another mega-nymphomaniac, Madame Bouvillon (p.121/81). Scarron's techniques often involved comic silhouettes and heavily emphasised sequential chains of activity, a manner which calls to mind today's animated cartoon films. The effects — squalid activity and grotesque comicality — combine to precipitate, at the end of Diderot's satirical section, the overall tone: intense interest, induced by attention-compelling vividness of imagery, inextricably mingled with scorn.

## 2. Irony: the paradox of the parasite

A further effect which Diderot wants to include is that of outrage. Two ingredients are commonly met with in eighteenth-century satire: the impudence of people who, judged by any sane criteria would be worthless, but who, thanks to their high opinion of themselves, are accepted by a foolish and uncritical public at their own inflated evaluation; and secondly, the misapplication of human ingenuity and resourcefulness to unworthy objectives of foolish triviality or of shameful viciousness. In these aspects of the satire the writer wants us to feel horror and revulsion at the topsy-turvy values of a money-dominated society, and to recognise in our hearts that what we are seeing, though a depressingly accurate representation of life and human energy as they probably are, is at the same time a travesty of society as it should be. The development of this kind of satire is the central theme of this section, which contains some strange ambivalences, double-thinking in which Lui argues both for the parasitic existence, and by occasional revelations of irony, against it.

Egged on by Moi, he develops a number of paradoxical aspects of the parasite's situation, beginning with the point that there is no flattery so gross that the host will reject it. He is thus deceived, and the parasite feels contempt for 'un grand sot...celui qui nous fête pour lui en imposer' (p.128/87). But why should the host thus allow them to bite the hand that feeds them? Lui's answer is, in essence, that there is no real deception here, since both hosts and parasites connive at the illusions. A casual observer might even think that there is a sort of familial consolation, a comforting 'école d'humanité' where failed authors, actresses and musicians can have their wounds licked and their spirits restored by the cohorts of sycophants who earn their meals by fawning on the untalented, and by skilfully decrying the truly great men, i.e. the *Encyclopédistes* and *philosophes* (Buffon, Duclos, Montesquieu, Rousseau, Voltaire, D'Alembert and Diderot (pp.129-30/88, compare p.111/74). But Lui makes it plain that any appearance of 'solidarity among parasites' is superficial: each is ready to betray the others, and expects in turn to be betrayed. It is here that Lui introduces the analogy, which will recur several times, of the ravening beasts ('des loups, des tigres') and the idea of the menagerie. It is believed that Madame de Tencin sets the fashion by referring to the habitués of her salon as her 'bêtes'. Lui's interpretation of the clique of parasites is much more penetrating and corrosive, however: the rascally hangers-on are like ferocious predators, each concerned only with acquiring money and meals. Throughout the development of this theme the 'jungle' parallels are pointed up by frequent allusions to zoos, cages, animals, 'espèces' etc.

The analysis of the host-parasite relationship, broken off temporarily, is resumed on page 140/96, where Lui elaborates on his idea of a 'pacte tacite qu'on nous fera du bien, et que tôt ou tard nous rendrons le mal pour le bien qu'on nous aura fait.' The host's motive in supporting the parasite is to disguise, through bribed help, some aspect of his own inadequacy, and to sustain some form of pretentious charlatanism. For example, Bertin has aspirations to be a playwright, and Hus, his mistress, claims to be an actress. The duties required of the parasite-protégé are therefore base and degrading: false adulation, the misleading of public opinion, gross and untruthful flattery of the hosts, servile attentions in place of true friendship or service. These characteristics have already been well illustrated in the accounts of services which Lui has rendered to 'le patron' and especially to Hus: we gather that it is his special duty to keep her happy (pp.120-23/80-83; 125-27/85-86; 138-39/95-96). Humiliated by these services, the parasite is justified in humiliating the host in return, by gossiping, publicly disclosing his weaknesses and absurdities. The host is well aware of this betrayal: because he is a sham himself, he can offer positions only to those sufficiently depraved to accept the degradation ('des âmes intéressées, viles et perfides'), and he knows that to expect anything other than disloyalty is against nature and 'le sens commun'; 'il y a je ne sais combien de noirceurs auxquelles il faut s'attendre' (pp.139-40/96-97).

Lui then launches on a splendidly sustained sequence of accusations focussed on Palissot, each showing — paradoxically

— that in all such treacheries the parasite is 'right', in that he is only acting in accordance with his nature as a vicious, unscrupulous, remorseless animal, while the victim is to blame, not only for expecting better treatment, but for associating with such a beast in the first place: 'Les honnêtes gens font ce qu'ils doivent; les espèces aussi, et c'est vous qui avez tort de les accueillir' (p.142/98). Thus, he concludes, the social parasites are agents of retribution, redressing the balance of justice, and acting on behalf of Providence or more likely, of Nature, which punishes with appropriate ailments and diseases those organisms which allow themselves to become degenerate (pp.142-43/ 98-99). We must therefore accept these conditions of existence, and either be upright 'honnêtes gens', and avoid contacts with unsavoury characters, or else resign ourselves to live as delinquents, preying and preyed upon according to the law of the jungle.

This is the end of Lui's argument. Two aspects invite comment. One is his acceptance, at this point in the book, of two parallel societies: that of the 'honnêtes gens', and that of the rogues or 'espèces'. He claims that it is possible for upright people to refuse to have any dealings with the rogues, and leaves us with a picture of a two-level social ecology in which the wicked could be conveniently ostracised and left to punish one another. This view is patently naive, as is Lui's claim that had Bertin and Hus been 'honnêtes', there would have been no scandalous tales to tell about them. It is, however, necessitated by and in keeping with the satirical process: behind the ironies, paradoxes and humour, a clearcut moral position must be readily perceptible to the reader, if he is to be persuaded by the satire, and not confused by the witticisms. We shall see, however, in another part of the book, that Diderot adopts a more worldly and pessimistic view, accepting that we are all (except perhaps for the few *philosophes*) *espèces*, fawning parasitically on one another in a single, anarchic symbiosis of intertwining personalities and objectives (pp.179/126-27). A second noteworthy feature of the satirical theme is in the suggestion of the presence of Diderot as author of the attack. If the parasites, like fleas, providentially punish their hosts for

being verminous, who bites the fleas? Who redresses the balance
of justice against the parasites? 'Vous', says Lui, referring for
the one and only time not to Moi, but to Diderot himself as the
satirist, 'vous qui nous peignez tels que nous sommes' (p.143/
98). The assertion links with Lui's earlier observation (p.132/90)
that, 'dans la société des méchants, où le vice se montre à
masque levé', you can at least learn to recognise your mis-
conceptions about life and to shed them.

### 3. Palissot

Charles Palissot de Montenoy, 1730-1814, is the target of the
heaviest satirical fire. Not only is he the subject of a string of
accusations (pp.140-42/96-98), but his name is linked to le
Renégat d'Avignon (p.145/100) with whom he shares second
place among those who have achieved 'le sublime en mal'. The
story of le Renégat d'Avignon has been traced to a real-life
incident (see *6*, pp.202-03), but one which is unconnected with
Palissot or with Avignon. Diderot has evidently changed the
setting in order to associate the act of wickedness more closely
with Palissot, who had been involved in 1757 in some shady
dealings in Avignon, including a suspicious bankruptcy. The
reasons for Diderot's animosity towards him form part of the
troubled story of the *Encyclopédie*, which began to appear in
1751. The years 1758-1762 were the most dangerous for the
future of this work, the great achievement of Diderot's life.
Seven volumes had appeared, but the remainder (there were
eventually thirty-five in all) were officially banned, though they
were being secretly printed. Opponents of the *philosophes*
stepped up their attacks in a fusillade of pamphlets, and it was at
the very blackest moment, in May 1760, that Palissot produced
the most publicised and widely effective of these attacks, *Les
Philosophes*. The play turned out to be a poor one, and ran for
only fourteen performances, but anticipatory interest had been
acute, and the first houses were overcrowded.

A glance at the plot will indicate the nature of the satire. It
owes much to Molière's *Les Femmes savantes*. A group of
*philosophes*, represented as parasitic and charlatan intellectuals,

attempts to gain influence over a rich, gullible middle-aged widow, Cydalise, who has cultural pretensions. Their aim is to bring about the marriage of her daughter, Rosalie, to one of their number, and thus to secure her dowry. Rosalie, who loves elsewhere, is rescued by the wits of Marthon, the serving maid, who introduces her lover, the valet Crispin, disguised as a *philosophe*, and disciple of Rousseau. He enters on all fours as an animal, and munches a lettuce while discoursing on the merits of a return to a primitive natural life. The other *philosophes* having approved of his ideas, Crispin reveals his true identity, thus exposing them as frauds.

The caricatural representation of Rousseau's critique of civilisation is the one well-known part of Palissot's otherwise forgettable play. However, the publicity which it generated was very disturbing, and the *Encyclopédistes* appealed to Voltaire to intervene on their behalf. But Voltaire had a private understanding with Palissot, who had always expressed admiration for him. In his *Petites Lettres*, he had placed Voltaire with Locke and Condillac as 'true' philosophers, and had attacked Diderot and his collaborators by contrast as bogus, and as deliberately misleading the public. Voltaire, while remaining superficially cordial to Diderot, refused to take up the cudgels, and turned his fire instead upon Fréron, and on others not named in *Le Neveu de Rameau*. The coolness of certain references to Voltaire (pp.84/51-52, 86/53, 86-88/54-55) is possibly attributable to Diderot's awareness of his relationship with Palissot. The reasons for attacking Palissot are now obvious. The only *philosophe* (other than Rousseau) clearly recognisable in the play is Diderot, as Dortidius (an anagram of Did'rot with a Latin ending added) shown as the unscrupulous leader of the plot to exploit Cydalise and Rosalie, and described as a 'charlatan de la philosophie' (*11*, line 635). Palissot had previously disrupted the unity of the *philosophes* as a group by clever mischief-making, and had contributed in varying ways and to varying degrees to the alienation from the *Encyclopédistes* of some major collaborators, such as Voltaire and Rousseau, and, in particular, D'Alembert, whom Diderot had greatly admired and relied upon, and who left the team of editors in 1757 under pressure of unpleasant publicity. *Les Philosophes* had come at a point of maximum danger for the future of the *Encyclopédie*, and it had cast a public slur on Diderot's professional and personal integrity, representing him as charlatan, ignoramus and unprincipled swindler of foolish women.

If we turn to look at the other people satirised in *Le Neveu de Rameau* we can understand the area of Diderot's attack as spreading outward from *Les Philosophes*.

## 4. Diderot's other targets: the web around Palissot

The most conspicuous of these attacks is that upon Adélaïde-Louise-Pauline Hus (1734-1805), probably because she was the most unpopular and the most vulnerable of the targets. After several attempts she gained a place in the Comédie Française in 1753, and she retained it until 1780. Gossip had it that she made her way by the influence of rich protectors, and evaluations of her acting ranged from unenthusiastic to condemnatory. Her liaison with Bertin lasted fifteen years, and was punctuated by frequent infidelities on both sides. It ended in 1761 about four months after the supposed April meeting between Moi and Lui, as a result of a complicated amorous adventure at Bertin's country house, involving a neighbouring landowner, Monsieur Viellard (p.93/59). Diderot had an inside account of it from Abbé Joseph Delaporte (the abbé who caused Lui's dismissal), and passed it on with great relish in a letter to Sophie Volland. We may speculate that Rameau, retained mainly as Mademoiselle Hus's supporter and minder, was got rid of in the course of Bertin's increasing disenchantment with her (see pp.136-37/93-94).

Lui delivers the attack in three passages, behind each of which we can discern the causes of Diderot's animosity, and his satirical tactics. In the first (pp.121-23/81-83) he refers to her vanity and stupidity, describing his ways of flattering her delusions that she was witty, intelligent and talented. He ensures that she wins arguments by bellowing support at precisely timed junctures, or by suggesting the overwhelming superiority of her reasoning by an elaborate sequence involving body-movement, shrugging and play of the hands. In real life, it seems, a rather similar role was played by Fréron (see *11*, pp.xvi-xvii) in brow-beating the reluctant assembly of the actors of the Comédie Française into putting on Palissot's play, and acting on behalf of Hus, whose name appears in the most flattering, but least demanding role, that of Rosalie.

The second passage (pp.126-28/85-87) explains how, in the presence of Hus, Lui has to pretend that two famous and widely acclaimed actresses, Mademoiselle Clairon and Mademoiselle Dangeville, are less gifted than she is, and Diderot very noticeably takes care that Lui's ironies do not mislead the reader: 'la supériorité des talents de la Dangeville et de Clairon est décidée' says Moi. Diderot's intentions are not hard to discern: in underlining Hus's lack of acting ability, he is advancing the view that she and the play are only being put on reluctantly, through bribed agents and unfair pressures. Thus, he refers to the other members of the Comédie Française in a complimentary and forgiving way: Dangeville, who had played Marton (see also p.138/95), Dumesnil (Cydalise) whose alcoholism and consequent unpredictability are gently indicated (p.106/69) and Préville, who played Crispin-Rousseau so successfully. It is odd, however, that he makes no mention of Clairon's courageous objection to the staging of the play, her refusal of a part in it, and her violent public protest at the first performance, when she berated her fellow members of the troupe, and threatened to resign (*11*, p.xviii). The mystery is increased by the lukewarm nature of references to her elsewhere in the book (e.g. p.106/69), despite the fact that she was well known for her support of the *philosophes*.

The final passage (pp.137-41/94-96) amplifies on the widely held belief that parts were found for Hus only through her protectors' financial influence, and develops the implication that Palissot's play is a further example of the same money-backed foisting of worthless products on a resentful public. Lui's comic portrayal of himself as a one-man claque adds another aspect to the same general point, and links with the view that the first performances of *Les Philosophes* were applauded by audiences mainly of wealthy or aristocratic families, with large numbers of their retainers, brought in for the purpose. 'C'est moi...qui l'ai fait applaudir' wrote Fréron (*11*, p.xvii, see also *3*, pp.198-201).

The Bertin involved in *Le Neveu de Rameau* is not to be confused with H.-L.-J.-B. Bertin d'Antilly, 1719-92, a very capable and respected administrator, who helped Diderot on at least two occasions: in 1759, at a delicate point in the fortunes of the *Encyclopédie*, and in 1774, in connection with the business affairs of Diderot's son-in-law. The Bertin with whom we are concerned was his cousin, Louis-Auguste Bertin de Blagny, dates unknown, but still alive in 1791. In 1742, having made a fortune as a tax-farmer, he bought the office of Trésorier des fonds particuliers du roi (Keeper of the Privy Purse) in the department of 'Parties casuelles' (Occasional Transactions). The title lent itself to jokes of the kind found on pages 127/86 and 143/99: in reality, Bertin's position was that of receiver of payments due to the Crown when offices in the judiciary or the administration of finances changed hands. It was a highly paid undemanding position which he held until its suppression in 1788.

Diderot's representation of him as pontificating mindlessly on cultural matters (p.131/89) is probably a distortion: he was a person of some refinement, a member of the Académie des Inscriptions, and author of several learned writings on financial and administrative institutions. He had, however, become noted in the gossip journals for his ostentation and his turbulent liaisons, often with actresses, and Diderot's portrayal of him as a frail, ill-tempered hypochondriac (pp.120-21/80) shamelessly attempting to buy people and exploit them, and the unkind anecdote suggesting impotence, echo the impression created by gossip. From information gleaned in the text, we can see that Diderot believed that the idea of *Les Philosophes* was conceived under his roof (p.130/88) and that Bertin had written *Les Philosophes de bois*, a successful adaptation of the jokes from Palissot's play, for marionettes. According to Diderot's friend Grimm, Bertin was helped in this by two well-known minor writers, Mouhy and Favart; according to others, however, it was not by Bertin, but by Louis Poinsinet de Sivry. Diderot's brilliant caricature of Bertin as a marionette-pagode (pp.120-21/81) is probably a retaliation against this piece, and it is also noticeable that, among the *anti-philosophe* writers, Poinsinet comes in for the third heaviest attack, after Palissot and Fréron (pp.89/55, 122/82, 140/97).

Apart from direct responsibility for the writing of *Les Philosophes* or its sequels, Diderot attacks Bertin for gathering around him writers and artists opposed to the *philosophes*. Some of those named are generally believed to have been friends or acquaintances of Diderot (for example, Abbé Delaporte, editor of the impartial journal, *Observateur littéraire*, Baculard d'Arnaud, and Robbé de Beauveset), and his only objection seems to have been that they attended Bertin's gatherings. The other three journals named on pages 134-35/92 were, however, hostile to the *philosophes*, and a central thread of Diderot's concern seems to be the power of finance over the media: book publishing, the Comédie Française, the press, and even the Opéra Comique. The forces of inertia, thus equipped, had a valuable publicity weapon in the struggle for the nation's opinion, and Diderot suggests something of the extent of the sinister network of financial power, by his attack on Bouret's brothers and son-in-law, P.G. Legendre de Villemorien, and D.P. Thiroux de Montsauge (pp.130/88, 142/98) who had also amassed large fortunes and made exalted family connections (see *3*, pp.194-95), and who were understandably committed to the defence of the existing political régime, against the liberal attitudes apparent in the *Encyclopédie*.

Behind the financiers were still more eminent enemies, to whom Diderot alludes more sparingly and obliquely. The Duc de Choiseul, who with Le Dauphin was commonly asserted to have supported or even ordered the performance of *Les Philosophes* (*11*, pp.xx-xxi), is alluded to (pp.81-82/50) as the 'ministre...qui démontra que rien n'était plus utile aux peuples que le mensonge'. The reference is to Choiseul's concern, as Secretary of State for War in the late 1750s, that the cosmopolitanism of the *philosophes*, and their ideas of the brotherhood of man, might sap nationalistic loyalties, and further demoralise the armed forces. The reason for Diderot's special satirical attention to Bouret (pp.123/83, 145/100, 180/127) is that he had actively supported Choiseul as a major financer of the campaign of 1756-60 against the *Encyclopédie*, and through his close connections with Machault, was an important link between high finance and political leaders.

## 5. Summing up: the paradox of the secret satire

To judge by the qualities of Diderot's attacking skills, his manner and his pace, the satirical section of *Le Neveu de Rameau* would, if he had published it, have succeeded in all its purposes: in capturing readers' interest, by entertaining them with personalities, anecdotes and humour; in vilifying Palissot, Bertin and Hus; in suggesting a menacing underworld of low life, linked with high finance, exploitation and deception; and in fostering uneasiness about national life, and possibly destabilising the régime. Moreover, considered at a purely stylistic level, it is brilliantly penned: the irony is carefully controlled so as not to misfire, and the main targets are delineated with sufficient clarity for there to be no ambiguity about the direction of the thrust. Diderot thus avoids two common faults in eighteenth-century satire, and he can also produce special effects, sometimes amounting to strokes of genius. My favourite is the interchange where Hus, acting as go-between, intercedes with Bertin, who replies only to her, ignoring Lui's presence (pp.136-37/93-94), and where Diderot leaves the reader to sense who speaks each of the lines; but there are a number of such finely tuned effects to choose from.

So why did Diderot let his satire lie unused, locked in his secret drawer, but taken out periodically and adjusted? Our survey of the substance suggests a possible explanation. In the first place, many of the influential people who had favoured Palissot were still alive when Diderot died in 1784. Although Bouret had died in disgrace in 1777, his name was linked with a number of wealthy and influential family connections. The two Bertins survived until the 1790s, and a published attack on Bertin de Blagny could not have failed to embarrass the respected Bertin d'Antilly, on whom Diderot depended for a favour in 1774. Moi's line 'Chacun a sa petite Hus et son Bertin' (p.179/127) could well have been coined on that occasion. In the second place, Palissot's fortunes and image declined sharply after 1762, and he lost his powerful protectors. Thirdly, from the same date, 1762, thanks to Malesherbes's discreet diplomacy, the authorities turned a blind eye to the re-emergence of the *Encyclopédie*, and to publish a noisy attack on Palissot would have been not only superfluous, but seriously counter-productive. It would have called attention to the still shaky legal position of the *Encyclopédie*'s publication, and it would have recalled the strong feelings of 1760, and embarrassed many who had since abandoned Palissot.

So we may conjecture that Diderot realised that, as a strategic missile, his blockbuster against Palissot and friends had become rapidly obsolete. But what was his reason for keeping it totally secret, even from his closest friends, to the very end of his life? No one knows, but perhaps it was the realisation that it was such a richly amusing and attractive work that, once revealed to one friend, he would be unable to withhold it from others, and that then the potent satirical element, once released, could produce a boomerang effect upon his fortunes and those of the *Encyclopédie*.

## 4. Genius

One of Diderot's gifts as a fiction writer is that of raising, around his central characters and stories, questions and ideas of universal and perennial fascination, which lend themselves to infinite debate, not only between characters in the tale, but also, as we gradually become aware, between Diderot as author, standing behind his narration, and ourselves as readers. In the case of *Le Neveu de Rameau*, Diderot takes as his leading subject the idea of genius. Whether it is the main theme of the book is not easy to decide, but it is certainly a central idea in terms of the structure of the work, because important further discussions branch out from it, and because echoes of it recur to the closing pages.

In presenting this theme, Diderot on several occasions uses techniques which have as a common characteristic delayed revelation, a feature worth noticing in passing since it is a form of narrative artistry which not only enhances the work, but also helps to link together unobtrusively the intermittent phases of the discussion. The leading in of the subject offers the first example (pp.79-81/48-49). Beneath the inconsequential banalities of the opening exchanges Moi gently pushes Lui towards talking about 'genius', no doubt intrigued to learn whether such a bizarre eccentric as he has just sketched in the introduction, imagines himself to be one. We can notice the recurrence of Moi's 'leading' words and phrases: '...ceux qui le poussent bien', 'hommes sublimes' ('sublime', meaning 'inspired' was an adjective particularly associated with discussions of genius in the eighteenth century), 'l'homme de génie', 'le sage'. And inevitably Lui, who lives in the shadow of his uncle's reputation, rises to the chance to speak of 'mon cher oncle'. A little further prompting has him launched on the topic of great men, and speaking knowingly of 'les gens de génie' (pp.82/50ff).

## *1. The value of the genius*

The discussion turns, not so much on the nature of genius in itself, but rather on the personalities of those who possess it, Lui contending that with their egocentric dedication to one particular activity, they are harmful to their families, friends, other social contacts, and indeed to humanity. As he sees it, they are gratuitous revolutionists: they discover new truths which change the face of the world and the course of history, but the social disruption, disturbance and distress which this involves far outweigh any theoretical or idealistic benefits of 'truth'. In practice, accepted illusions and false beliefs are more useful to the masses and less damaging. Furthermore, the genius harms society if, like Socrates, he sets an example of law-breaking, and he is also damaging to himself if, like Racine, he gets little money for his work, and cannot live in style, with an entourage of hangers-on. All of which leads Lui to conclude that if it were possible to detect genius at birth, all such infants should be destroyed (pp.82/50, 83/51).

Moi accepts the same basic assumptions about the behaviour of geniuses, but takes the conventional view that they are beneficial. However unpalatable and disconcerting their new discoveries are in the short term, truth is always advantageous in the long run. Thus, geniuses advance the development of the human species as a whole, and posterity honours the ages and the nations which produce them. Developing the idea that, with the genius, the apparent revolution is in fact evolution, Moi differentiates between two kinds of law, the one 'd'une équité, d'une généralité absolues', i.e. universal and eternal justice, which he seems to think is represented in the judgement of posterity, and which will discern the 'rightness' of the genius and his 'truth'. The other kind is the man-made temporal and local law, laws which may be made to meet particular circumstances, and which may be unjust in the long run, or even downright wrong-headed and tyrannical. This second type of law may cover the offender with ignominy (as in Socrates's case), but should he subsequently prove to be a genius, posterity will exonerate the 'criminal', and condemn the blindness and narrowness of his nation, his age, and its law-givers.

This leads to a crucial admission by Moi: genius is often associated with a touch of madness ('un grain de folie'), and this can in some cases take the form of wickedness ('méchanceté'). But, he adds, the evil done by the genius is limited: although the lives of his personal and social contacts may be ruined, this evil is far outweighed by the good he brings, because the whole of humanity, in its succeeding generations, will benefit from his discoveries (p.86/53).

Taken in themselves, these points seem to add up to a fairly conventional view of genius, but taken in conjunction with Lui's side of the case they open up two possibilities of major significance for the subsequent development of the book. One is the problem posed by originality: genius (for example, that of Socrates) might not be readily apparent to its own generation, to current systems of values and laws: it may only become manifest in retrospect, to later ages. This means that genius might exist in as yet unrecognised fields of activity. The way is prepared for Lui's display of genius in musical mimes. The second possibility is that a genius remains an evolutionary asset to humanity, and therefore one whose existence should be preserved, even if he is a wicked and anti-social person. The way is prepared for Lui's justification of genius in parasitism, that is to say, in the field of the despicable or the inconsequential. The way is also prepared for the contemplation of 'le sublime dans le mal': genius displayed in the field of criminality.

Now that we have this skeleton of ideas and their development in our minds, it is possible to come back to the text, and to see how Diderot has conducted the discussion, not in terms of abstract ideas and argument-building, but in terms of concrete realities: situations of various kinds, comic, dramatic, pornographic; anecdotes and intrigues of elaborate deviousness; people with strange gifts, motivations and vices. What is more, the concoction is based on real persons, events and scandals, and laced with Diderot's scathingly satirical asides. For instance he creates for himself the opportunity to snipe at a couple of notable contemporaries by making Lui and Moi delay in agreeing on examples. Moi rejects Lui's choice, J.-P. Rameau who, though well qualified in unamiable selfishness, might not prove to be a genius in the eyes of posterity, and Voltaire, suggested by Moi, is rejected by Lui on similar grounds.

Though polite to Voltaire in public, since he was a fellow *philosophe*, Diderot privately disliked his spitefulness to rivals, his sly but persistent self-advertisement, and, of course, his 'secret' encouragement of Palissot. They finally accept Racine, who had made up for a very unpleasant childhood by becoming a very unpleasant adult, and who, like Diderot, was a native of Langres where a portrait, said to be of him, gazes balefully from the walls of the Musée with sensual but soulful sadism. It is Moi who poses the challenging question: Would it have been better if Racine had been a solid citizen, totally worthy but pedestrian, like Brianson (publisher of the *Encyclopédie*) or Barbier (a successful draper of the 'sixties, specialising in up-market fashion fabrics), or if he had been what he was, namely the author of *Britannicus* and other uplifting and immortal plays, and withal a treacherous, lecherous wretch?

Before the question is answered, a number of interesting incidental skirmishings flower from it: Moi, for example, wonders whether geniuses, without their faults, would still have been able to fulfil their potential; Lui wonders why Nature could not have created them morally good as well as great, but accepts (and will later exploit) Moi's rejoinder that evil is necessary in the Universe, that good could not exist without its opposite, and that each person must fulfil his own individual nature. On balance we are left with a favourable view of Racine, because Diderot gives Moi a rich simile to describe his position: it is that of a fine tree, which stifles a few saplings around it, but affords shade, beauty and fruits to many centuries to come. The point that Moi had earlier formulated in abstract terms, that the genius is an essential factor in the progress of the human race, and must be allowed to live, however wicked, has now been supported and conveyed in terms of real examples and imagery. A momentary victory for Moi, perhaps, but a reinforcement of the springboard for the claims which Lui will make in the subsequent phases of the debate.

## 2. *Genius in the despicable: parasitism as a fine art*

The next major stage in the discussion of genius is provided by
the disaster which has just befallen Lui, a tale which Diderot
gradually lets out, at the same time slowly building up the
substance of Lui's claim to be a genius in parasitism. From the
faintest of preoccupations ('ce n'est rien...', p.88/55)
indications become by degrees more explicit: 'Ce qui m'afflige
aujourd'hui...' etc., until by pages 91-92/58 we gather that he
has lost his comfortable place in a rich man's household, but we
do not learn the full story until much later (pp.135-37/92-94).
Similar tantalising techniques are used elsewhere in Diderot's
fiction, for example in *Jacques le fataliste*. Here in *Le Neveu de
Rameau* the delay serves a discernible purpose in relation to the
ideas, for it allows Diderot to dwell at some length on the
characteristics which the Hus household valued in Lui: these are
the list of vices and failings of which he boasts ('...je suis un
ignorant...' etc.) to the amusement of Moi, and which make him
an entertaining and irreplaceable hanger-on. His various skills
are analysed (in essence they consist of being amusing, useful,
yet 'sans conséquence'), and illustrated with mimes: he is
incomparable in the arts of grovelling, of encouraging bashful
young men, and of procuring young girls for them.

Diderot further exploits the delay in the revealing of the
crucial dismissal, to establish the existential self-hood of Lui. As
he goes over his painful experience, he oscillates with increasing
violence between self-aggrandisement and self-contempt, and it
is amusing to follow through Diderot's technique in building up
this progressive dither (pp.87-94/54-59). From self-reproach he
skips to an imaginary revelling in the wealth, power and inward
satisfaction which would have been his had he possessed his
uncle's musical gifts, and entertains Moi with the first mime of
the book: himself as rich, celebrated, and fawned upon by
spongers. He proceeds unashamedly to list his despicable
characteristics, considering them as qualities with which he has
been endowed 'à un rare degré', only to veer back to self-
reproach for having lost his post. After further waverings, the
sequence culminates in the disclosure of the inner force which

drives Lui: 'une certaine dignité attachée à la nature de
l'homme, que rien ne peut étouffer' (pp.93-94/59), but which is
intuitive, irrational, unpredictible and intermittent, for at
another moment, he admits, he would accept the humiliation
without demur, a reflection which leads Lui and Moi into a
learned debate upon the spiritual significance of kissing
Mademoiselle Hus's backside. A final stage of the sequence
links Lui's pride to that of the artist-genius: he is tormented by
'le mépris de soi-même', not through any normal dignity, but
because he considers himself vastly superior in inventiveness and
skill to many who have made fortunes as parasites, and suffers
pangs of a strange remorse, not for wickedness, but for not
using his talents: 'l'inutilité des dons que le Ciel nous a départis'
(pp.96/61-62).

The discussion, temporarily discontinued, is completed on
pages 119-134/80-91. Diderot makes it clear that he is picking up
the subject at the point where it was left off by referring to the
memorable obeisance, as Moi again advises Lui to ingratiate
himself with Hus, and Lui refers again to his 'dignité'. It is in
this sequence that Lui's claim to genius eventually and by
degrees becomes explicit. Hitherto it has been adumbrated but
not voiced. Describing in detail the resources of flattery and
diplomacy required in those who dance attendance on the
imperious, capricious Hus, he claims to have brought to this
difficult and delicate role an adroitness, a professional expertise,
which is unique: 'Personne n'a eu cet art comme moi...',
'Personne ne m'a surpassé...' A little later we find him boasting
that he has studied the work of satirists and moralists, like
Theophrastus, La Bruyère and Molière, for their valuable
portraits of the typical hypocrite, miser, swindler etc., so that he
can indulge in these vices, but at the same time guard against
looking like the stock image, and thus avoid detection and
retribution. By such researches he claims to have re-defined and
instituted the art of cadging, 'd'avoir fait par système, par une
vue raisonnable et vraie, ce que la plupart des autres font par
instinct' (pp.133-34/91), and as a final display of virtuosity he
gives a dazzling example of the court jester's mock-Aristotelian
logic.

In the course of this sequence, which is amplified in order to serve its parallel purpose of satirising Hus and Bertin, Moi asks Lui 'avec cette fertilité de génie est-ce que vous n'avez rien inventé?'. Lui lists his 'inventions' referring back to mimes or suggested mimes earlier in the book, and ending '...si cela était écrit, je crois qu'on m'accorderait quelque génie.' But why should he write it down, he asks: 'Les génies lisent peu, pratiquent beaucoup, et se font d'eux-mêmes'. In support he cites three military leaders, and three socially prominent figures of the day, whose careers might be described as masterpieces of cynical exploitation. The incident is of importance in preparing for the ambivalence of the discussion of Lui's genius towards the end of the book, for it indicates that Diderot is at least prepared to consider the possibility of genius existing in the field of practical activities, without insisting that the productions be recorded in permanent form.

## 3. Genius in evil

Intertwined with Lui's claim to genius in parasitism, and with the satire of Bertin, Hus and Palissot, is a section of the book bristling with mysteries, the discussion of 'le sublime en mal' (pp.123-49/83-103). The central theory is clear enough: extreme wickedness has an epic quality: the petty offender is contemptible, but 'on ne peut refuser une sorte de considération à un grand criminel.' Genius in evil is the highest of attainments: 'il importe d'être sublime, surtout en mal!' (p.144/100). Lui places in order of excellence four potential claimants for the title of 'King of Criminals' (*fourbum Imperator*): they are, in first place, Etienne Michel Bouret, then, as equal seconds, Palissot (satirised particularly pp.140-42/96-98) and Le Renégat d'Avignon (pp.145-48/100-03), and modestly taking fourth place, himself. By today's standards of atrocity, when ogre-like dictators, blood baths, systematic genocide, chemical- and germ-warfare, total annihilation of humanity and most other forms of life have become familiar and distinct possibilities, all the crimes described by Lui seem anodine by comparison, but one feels that even so, living as he did in an age which had its fair share of violence and persecution Diderot might have produced more impressive horrors. However, such pedestrian criticisms are clearly out of place, since the order of achievement is intentionally perverse.

The worst of the crimes is probably that of Le Renégat, and the least reprehensible is self-evidently that of Bouret, who is nevertheless awarded the title for nothing more dastardly than a confidence trick worked on a dog, in which, according to Lui, the use of a mask represents the ultimate in inspired subterfuge (pp.123-25/83-85). It is difficult to guess at Diderot's intention here. We can see, of course, the satirical reason for the inclusion of the anecdote. Bouret had made an immense fortune in the Tax Farms, as investor, then as administrator, helped by the protection of Jean-Baptiste de Machault d'Arnouville, Contrôleur général des finances, 1745-54, Garde des Sceaux i.e. Ministre de la Justice, 1750-54, and Secrétaire d'Etat de la Marine, 1754-57. Machault was the receiver of the dog. The incident was recounted in *L'Espion anglais* of January 1774, but the date of its occurrence is uncertain. Its significance in the structure of the discussion of genius is very difficult to explain satisfactorily. It might be meant to suggest that the stroke of supreme genius, if accomplished in a new or unconventional field, will (like the merit of Socrates, or the great mime of Lui) pass unappreciated by all but a few connoisseurs, because most people, including the reader, will not be able to discern any brilliance in it (as here, for example, in the use of the mask) and will probably dismiss it as trite, a waste of time and effort.

Diderot could have intended the incident to act on the reader's mind in this way, for as Fabre's notes show, Bouret was indeed a bold innovator in the art of ostentatious showmanship and ingratiating oneself with the King. Lui's allusions to 'Le Livre de la Félicité' and the *flambeaux* (p.123/83) refer to Louis XV's visit to Bouret's château, which he publicised by having the road back to Versailles lit, for the passing of the King's carriage, by peasants and other estate workers standing with torches at thirty-yard intervals. For this same event, he had printed and richly bound, for presentation to the King, a sort of diary entitled 'Le Vrai Bonheur', of some fifty pages, each bearing only the words 'Today the King visited Bouret', and awaiting the addition of the date, which the King was slow to fix. It is also possible that Diderot, realising that any attempt to produce a straightforward example of consummate artistry in sycophancy would probably fall flat, offered Bouret, a financier grown excessively rich and well known through tax-exploitation, as a token example, purposely facetious, and left it to the reader to perceive the drift of the argument.

Indications that he might have deliberately trivialised the story can be found by comparing it with the report in *L'Espion anglais*, quoted by Fabre, *3*, p.195. There is no mention of 'le masque', and Diderot's version shows other signs of adaptation.

The story of Le Renégat d'Avignon seems to have been included mainly for purposes of satirising Palissot, and adds little to the theorising about genius, but it is, unlike the other tales of villainy, sufficiently horrifying to justify Moi's revulsion at Lui's approval and scholarly appreciation of 'le sublime en mal' at the close of the section, and sufficiently ingenious to justify also the fact that Moi, in his aside, cannot gainsay Lui's thesis that 'genius' can reasonably be said to exist, even in 'la méchanceté' (pp.148-49/103-04).

## 4. Lui: a genius?

The final re-emergence of the theme of genius comes on pages 170-74/119-22. Diderot leaves the discussion unresolved, but maps out two broad areas of alternative interpretation, so that the dialogue can go on in the reader's consciousness. Moi opens the encounter by suggesting strongly to Lui that he should create something: 'Dites-moi comment il est arrivé que...vous n'avez rien fait qui vaille?' Lui replies that Nature has given him only one talent: that of conjuring money out of the pockets of the gullible; but Moi persists: why not write 'un bel ouvrage' on the methods and skills of cadging? Lui wavers momentarily: he has tried writing many times, only to realise that far from being a genius, 'je suis un sot', and he dissolves in a cloud of excuses, beginning and ending on the theme 'poverty kills inspiration'. He declares that he will resign himself to being what Nature has destined him for: a practising parasite, not a theorising one, cajoling a living from an over-rich society, joining in the fawning, servile dance of inter-dependency... (pp.177-78/125).

One possible interpretation of this sequence is that talents, gifts, ability, no matter how great, can never ripen into genius without courage, self-discipline, the resolute and obstinate will to create, to stick single-mindedly to the objective, whatever the difficulties. This is a quality which Lui has admitted all along to be lacking in himself, at least as far as writing is concerned: 'Alors je me sentais du courage, l'âme élevée, l'esprit subtil, et capable de tout. Mais ces heureuses dispositions apparemment ne duraient pas...' (p.96/61, compare p.126/85-86). The quotation from Horace which heads the book, referring to Vertumnis, god of change in the weather and seasons, seems to tie in with this picture of Lui as inconstant, unreliable, unstable.

But Diderot does not end the book with Lui's admission of being unable to write, and Lui does not slink off defeated: he departs still bearing the burden of his great potential gifts, and the torment of 'l'inutilité des dons'. And Diderot has, intriguingly, left within the discussion of genius another thread, another possible interpretation.

If Lui has left some of his gifts undeveloped, there are others on which he has lavished boundless energy and dedicated self-discipline. 'Le temps s'est écoulé', he says, 'et c'est toujours autant d'amassé' (pp.98-99/62-63). Among other gains, the wrist, which was once stiff and unskilled, has become marvellously supple and capable — of performing on violin or harpsichord perhaps (Diderot does not tell us), but certainly of *miming* such performances with supreme exactitude, indeed with genius. It is relevant in this connection to look back at the series of mimes on pages 88-100/55-65, and to notice the progression of Moi's comments on his reactions to them. The first and second mimes represent Lui's skills as sycophant and procurer, and Moi simply describes the actions and situations, conveying their detail and accuracy, but nothing more. But with the third (pp.96-97/62) he is not only amused, but torn between admiration at Lui's skill, and outrage at the corruption represented. That is to say, he is experiencing the same emotions as he might have had, if witnessing the reality. The following mimes make the point more forcibly still, for they represent musical performances. Moi's comments register not only the preciseness of Lui's observations and portrayals, but the fact that the performances arouse in him the same feelings and awareness of beauty as the real performance: 'Il est sûr que les accords résonnaient dans ses oreilles *et dans les miennes*', says Moi, despite the fact that, as he later confesses, he was not musical enough to recognise the particular pieces rendered.

These two mimes, of violinist and harpsichordist, herald the major and central mime of the book (pp.156-59/108-11), where again the musical effect on all hearers was the equivalent of that of a real performance. The point is finally re-stated on page 170/119, when Moi explicitly recognises the true quality of Lui's unusual genius, and reminds him of his amazing 'facilité de sentir, de retenir et de rendre les plus beaux endroits des grands maîtres, avec l'enthousiasme qu'ils vous inspirent, *et que vous transmettez aux autres*'. And Lui in turn recognises the one odd mutation of *le fibre* which he has inherited from his forebears: 'Le fibre m'a manqué, mais le poignet s'est dégourdi; l'archet marche et le pot bout. Si ce n'est pas de la gloire, c'est du bouillon' (p.173/122, compare p.98/63).

According to this second interpretation, instead of dismissing Lui as a failed would-be genius, Diderot might be suggesting that he is a genius in spheres not recognised by contemporary culture: in parasitic skills, and in musical mime. In both these fields, Lui has shown not only the magic of inspiration, and the fertility of original invention but also the dedicated tenacity of purpose in cultivating suppleness of limbs and body, expressiveness of vocal chords and of posture. All he lacks is a cultural context of critical evaluation and comment. Hence, unlike the genius in normal acting or normal music-making, his attainments, superb though they are, will go unrecorded and unacclaimed. Diderot realised that the brilliant mimes *could* be recorded and evaluated, at least in his own favoured form of story-telling, based on real people and happenings, a form which we might call 'sub-fiction'. He has rendered this service to J.-F. Rameau, perhaps in response to a genuine and uplifting musical experience, received in the course of a memorable conversation.

The proposition created in the reader's mind by the two alternative judgements of Lui: non-genius, through lack of persistence? or genius, but in unaccepted spheres? is a fascinating one. What, we may wonder, would have happened to the genius of — say — Chaplin, Tati or Ustinov, had they lived in the eighteenth instead of the twentieth century? What geniuses are today struggling in fields we have not yet acknowledged? Are there evil geniuses at work, undetected beneath their finely calculated hypocrisies? Are some kinds of genius doomed perpetually to non-acceptance? What kind of genius did Diderot see as his own? Questions and speculations open out infinitely from the tension between the alternatives, a tension which is part of the enduring freshness of Diderot's book.

## 5. *Money,* Métier *and the Discussion of Morality*

It is apparent that the linked questions of morality, liberty, responsibility and happiness are at the heart of the book, for it is on this theme that the discussion ends. It is also apparent, however, that the direction and intention of Diderot's thinking beneath the multiple lines of argument taken by the two protagonists, are obscure: possibly he wished to illustrate the point that conversations of this philosophical kind are seldom conclusive. This means that we, as readers, must be prepared to examine and interpret the material to an even greater extent than with the more clearly oriented elements, those concerned with music, satire, and the question of genius. This in turn means that we should be more than ever careful to discern and make use of any structural features or signposts which might indicate Diderot's shaping of the writing. Let us start by noticing that there are three such signposts, in the form of three possible places at which Diderot might have ended the dialogue. They identify, and separate, points which he was concerned to establish, and by following through, from the earlier pages, the arguments which lead up to each of these points, we can to some extent disentangle and clarify the several intertwining threads which together make up the discussion of morality.

### 1. Money

In the first of the possible endings (p.169/119) Lui presents a definition of 'une bonne éducation': that which leads to all forms of enjoyment, without danger or difficulties. Moi accepts this, but only as a form of words: if they were to specify the 'périls et les inconvénients à éviter', they would no longer be in agreement. This summing up of the two positions could have served as an ending, because it would have left the reader with the two opposing sides of the argument clearly in mind, and with a sense of balance: Moi holds a fairly conventional view, while Lui's understanding of dangers and difficulties has just been explored in depth in relation to the education he is planning for his infant son, 'le petit sauvage'.

The sequence (pp.163-69/114-19) begins with an obviously worded change of subject from music to morality, in which Lui is going to present his case against idealism in morality and 'les charmes de la vertu'. The major theme in Lui's argument is money. Education, he claims, should teach its over-riding value: 'L'or est tout, et le reste, sans or, n'est rien', he cries, showing Moi how he struts and postures in front of his child, worshipping a gold coin. Around this theme Lui proposes educational principles which seem unassailable in themselves, but controversial in his way of applying them. One principle is that education should be geared to the times and moral values in which the child will have to live, and since contemporary society is largely composed of immoral, money-dominated people, it is cruelly misleading to equip him with an austere, noble, upright outlook, such as that of ancient Sparta (Lacedaemon). Lui is calling for 'idées d'institution calquées sur nos mœurs' — Moi's words, and a kind of admission (pp.166-67/116-17).

Secondly, education should take account not only of environment, but of heredity. It should not try to counteract individual characteristics by imposing a standard syllabus and behavioural guide. Should his son show signs of being 'un homme de bien', Lui would not oppose it, but if, as he hopes, he has inherited from 'la molécule paternelle' the ability to be a 'vaurien', Lui will train him to be a great one: for the worst outcome of education is to produce mediocrities, herd-creatures: 'des espèces (p.164/114-15). This individualistic élitism, existential and liberal to the point of anarchism, is matched with a third principle: amoralism and freedom from guilt feelings. The aim of education must be to enable one to live with oneself, unhypocritically, and to avoid self-condemnation or condemnation by society's opinion, behaviour patterns, or laws: Lui will teach his son 'la juste mesure, l'art d'esquiver à la honte, au déshonneur et aux lois', i.e. to sail just the right side of these 'périls et inconvénients' of conscience and convention (p.167/117-18). Moi's objections, few and mild, serve to underline the animalism and lawlessness implicit in Lui's views: suppose Lui's son, unrestrained by moral guidance, steals from his father, or yields to an Oedipus impulsion? Such things, replies Lui, though inconvenient, are at least 'dans la nature...de l'homme', which is more than Moi can claim for the opposing position, disdain of riches, which is present in only a few 'gens bizarres' (p.169/118, compare pp.115-16/77).

So this first possible ending point presents a balanced impasse: if Lui's side of the argument is more amply and closely argued, it is (or was in the eighteenth century), more unusual and revolutionary than Moi's conventional ideas, and therefore called for more explanation. The tresses of the argument leading up to this impasse can now be picked out from the earlier discussion of morality. The idea of the importance of money has been presented in a variety of forms: there are, firstly, a number of variations on the theme 'time is money': 'Un jour de moins à vivre, ou un écu de plus, c'est tout un' (p.97/62) says Lui, ushering in the section on moral issues; 'c'était autant d'argent et de temps épargné', he claims, if his pupil, having learned nothing, has no errors to un-learn; or again: 'si l'on me fait attendre, je crie comme si l'on me volait un écu' (pp.105/69, 107/71). Another theme is the claim that large fortunes can be amassed only by dishonesty, that riches can buy both an undeserved good name, and the unfair ruin of somebody else's good name; that society is corrupted, not by ordinary tricks of the trade and commercial sharpness, but by those who have an all-consuming, unceasing dedication to the making of money, 'gens toujours dans leurs boutiques'; that in 'stealing' the fee for a poorly-given music lesson, Lui, like other parasites, is only redressing the balance of justice in nature and society (pp.110-12/72-74). There are close similarities between these themes, and those encountered in relation to Diderot's satire: compare pages 129-30/88, 142-43/98. This re-emergence or intertwining of themes in *Le Neveu de Rameau* is referred to by some critics as 'tressing'.

The other collection of themes which lead up to the statements on pages 169-70/119 is that of educational values, aims and syllabuses. It forms a secondary parallel to the theme of money, and is not quite so coherently continued from its earlier appearances (see especially pp.100-05/65-68) into the concluding pages (pp.163/114 ff). The ideas are oddly out of place in Diderot's work, because they attack the traditional, encyclopaedic view of education as primarily the feeding in of information (grammar, history, geography etc.), accompanied by the development of rational thinking ('à raisonner juste') and moral principles, especially of the stoical and self-disciplining kind ('à supporter [les peines de la vie] avec courage'). These are the proposals put forward by Moi for his daughter's education, but Lui rejects them, using powerful arguments: academic subjects, like physics, mathematics and harmony (i.e. the theoretical side of music) are seldom if ever well taught, because the teacher would have to study for a lifetime before being able to give a proper explanation of the rudiments, their significance in relation to the subject as a whole, and the significance of the subject (e.g. physics) in relation to the structure of the universe (pp.103-05/67-68). Lui recommends instead practical skills (harpsichord playing, dancing, singing) which will make the girl more seductive: the other, cerebral studies will be at best useless, and could be positively dangerous. All that matters is that 'elle soit jolie, amusante et coquette'.

This attack on the values of the *Encyclopédie* may have been intended by Diderot to be taken in the same inconsequential way as the jokes made about Moi's appearance as an eccentric and shabby intellectual (pp.101-02/65-66, compare p.168/118), but it seems to go deeper than these flippancies. The point is worth noting, because we shall find other signs of self-questioning and soul-searching as we look at the other possible endings of the dialogue. This self-criticism has been taken by a number of critics to be the main function of *Le Neveu de Rameau*, which they see as a painfully honest dialogue with self, and possibly an unfavourable re-appraisal of Diderot's life's work and guiding principles.

However the attack is not pursued when the subject of education is resumed in the concluding pages, and we hear no more about academic subjects from Moi, while Lui rejects even practical music-making as a training for his son, despite Moi's (ironic) pleading that giving lessons would provide ready access to the homes of the rich, and a chance to exploit them. Lui, it seems, considers music useful only as a feminine accomplishment (pp.165-66/116): for the male *vaurien* he can teach faster and more certain methods of living off the rich.

## 2. *Métier*

The second possible ending-point (p.180/127) is associated with the celebrated culminating symbol of the book, the dance of dependency or 'pantomime des gueux', 'pantomime' being used here in its meaning of 'expressive movements of face and body, designed to convey motive, feeling or story'. According to Lui, it involves the whole of humanity, while for Moi, 'le philosophe qui n'a rien et qui ne demande rien' can be free from the web of dependency upon others. So once again we have an impasse in the argument, where neither side will concede anything, and hence a kind of balance, which could have formed the ending.

Lui's version of the dance of the beggars (pp.176-79/124-26) is ushered in with the description of the characteristic cringing posture of 'l'homme nécessiteux', and the view that in the 'diable d'économie' of an affluent society, whole sectors — the parasites — could not survive without cadging. There are several comparisons, similes intended mainly, it seems, for decorative purposes: an allusion to the new, expressive dance-positions introduced into ballet in Paris of the 1750s by the ballet-master J.G. Noverre, in an attempt (vain as it turned out) to liberate choreography from classical restrictions. Bonnet (*2*, pp.190-97) gives an interesting extract in which Noverre indicates his involvement with Diderot. Another comparison, not particularly apt or helpful, is to the leaking casks (p.174/122-23) which the daughters of King Danaus were condemned to fill eternally: by 'le tonneau percé', Lui means to imply that the parasite must catch the odd sporadic trickle of wealth inadvertently squandered by the rich, and thus has no security or independence. The main image is, however, soon re-affirmed: Nature, says Lui, could not have intended him to starve, for she has equipped him well for the role of jester or sponger, and he displays for Moi his proficiency in postures, and his gifts as an 'excellent pantomime'.

As Lui understands it, his 'danse des gueux' symbolises the predicament of the parasite at all levels, not exclusively the very poor: 'Voilà ma pantomime, à peu près la même que celle des flatteurs, des courtisans, des valets et des gueux'. Lui has produced a number of mimes illustrating fawning adulation and base servility, beginning with that on page 89/55, and particularly related to the satirical section. He has, moreover, produced anecdotes and explanations of the parasite's situation, frequently making the point that he, unlike the other hangers-on, is not a hypocrite (pp.96-97/61-62; 116-17/77-78; 132/90; 144/99; 167/117), acknowledging his own depravity, along with that of his fellow sycophants, and analysing it from within.

Thus, Lui's version of the dance makes an effective concluding concentration of imagery from the satirical section, a function which Diderot neatly exploits through Moi's suggestive private reflections on it (pp.178-79/126): the disrespectful humour of Rabelais or Galiani, like that of the Comédie Italienne, provides consolatory therapy for any reader who feels bruised by the arrogance of the wealthy; moreover, the playing of parts like that of the pedantic, wealthy establishment figure, Pantaloon, involved the wearing of masks, often with long nose-pieces, decorated to resemble animal faces: *pourceau, autruche, oie,* thinks Moi, reminding us of the imagery of the opponents of the *Encyclopédie,* as predatory, unscrupulous 'espèces'.

At this point, Moi introduces an adjustment to the interpretation of the *danse*: Lui has so far said nothing of the possible non-dancers, the victims of the parasites, 'l'imbécile et l'oisif' (p.110/73), the 'honnêtes gens' (pp.142-43/98-99). Moi now explicitly extends the symbolism to include everyone, even 'le souverain'. Lui accepts this readily, for the preparation of the adjustment lies in arguments put forward by himself earlier, in the theory of 'idiotismes du métier' (pp.107-10/70-73). Just as in language there are general rules of grammar and construction, and at the same time, turns of phrase or idioms, accepted by custom and usage, which depart from the general rules, so in morality there are general, nation-wide standards of honesty, and within each profession or trade, departures from these norms, petty deceptions which have become accepted by tradition as 'tricks of the trade'. We gather that the practices covered by the term 'idiotismes' range in seriousness from showmanship and advertiser's licence, through to sharp practice and illicit 'perks'. But although a measure of confidence-trickery is involved in all cases, Lui claims that the 'idiotismes' still give the customer better value when properly understood: 'il n'y a que le coup d'œil qu'il faut avoir juste'.

The point is illustrated through the two versions of his harpsichord lesson. When he was a novice, inexperienced in teaching, his lessons were obsequiously given and ill received. But now, in the second version, he arrogantly hectors his pupil, and pretends that his time is valuable and not to be wasted. In this later form, but not in the first, his lessons are, he contends, worth his fee: his claims to be important and sought after, though lies, create respect, and pupil and parents profit the more by his services.

The shrewdness of Lui's observations, and his distinction between 'business deceptions', little more than acumen, on the one hand, and corruption on the other (those who are 'opulents et estimés', 'toujours dans leurs boutiques', acquiring vast fortunes 'Dieu sait comment', pp.108-10/71-73) lead the reader to suspect that Diderot, as opposed to 'Moi', might regard Lui's view as the more realistic. In support of this, we may recall Diderot's theory of theatre, in which 'conditions' (i.e., one's place in society, including métiers) were supposed to carry distinctive moral obligations.[2]

Diderot seems to have felt, here in *Le Neveu de Rameau*, that the 'conditions' also carried permissive characteristics of deception and persuasion, for he includes several lists of conditions, each of which involve some measure of ostentation or easy living (pp.108/71, 110/73, and compare pp.134-35/92, where prominent figures in the worlds of entertainment, speculation and publicity are indicated). These lists are recalled

---

[2] *Entretiens sur Le Fils naturel*, in Diderot, *Œuvres esthétiques*, textes établis avec introductions, bibliographies et notes, par Paul Vernière, Classiques Garnier, 1959, pp.153-54.

by the wording of Moi's description of the *danse* as 'le grand branle de la terre' (p.179/126-27), and Diderot skilfully exploits this well-prepared theme to make his final scathing allusions to the sinister role of high finance in its defence of a rotting establishment, and its insidious links with the Church, through Lui's miming of the appropriate obsequious behaviour: Bouret making desperate pleas to the Contrôleur général des finances, when his financial empire was on the point of collapse; the Bishop of Orleans paying money in the laundered form of benefices from livings, to the servile Gauchat, for writing attacks on the *Encyclopédie*.

If Lui accepts Moi's first adjustment of the dance of dependency to include everyone, he objects strongly to a second adjustment, in which the *philosophe* is held to be able to detach himself from the network of cajolery (pp.180-81/127-28). The grounds for Lui's objection have been established a few pages earlier: it is all very well, he says, for Moi to take a distanced view, as if from the planet Mercury, classing man as intrinsically different from the rest of animal- and insect-creation. Lui claims to see things realistically, to live 'dans ce monde', 'terre à terre', where 'l'espèce humaine' struggles, like all other species, desperately but creatively, for individual survival.

These pages add a disturbing new ambivalence to the term 'espèce': used in the satirical section, it stigmatised the degraded brutality of the mercenary writers, indifferent to truth and ideals, like Palissot and friends; used on pages 164/114-15, it had signified the mediocrity induced by a standardising education, a herd mentality which Lui had associated with Diderot's rationalistic, encyclopaedic, and moral ideas on pedagogy. Now, as it is used in the phrase 'l'espèce des hommes' (p.177/125) it evokes a grandiose vision of human animals, struggling forward in a dynamic, infinitely diverse, competitive surge of vitality, in an inventive but totally undirected or unpredictable pattern of social evolution. Thus, two conflicting evaluations of man and his destiny are brought into balanced conjunction: Lui's view of biological anarchism, and Moi's view, of the stoical, virtuous but outcast *philosophe*, moralist and idealist, disdaining the majority of his fellow men and misunderstood by them, but possibly, like Socrates, able to lift humanity one step higher in its evolution, and to be appreciated by posterity.

## 3. Morality

Let us now look at the third possible ending: 'Les choses de la vie ont un prix, sans doute; mais vous ignorez celui du sacrifice que vous faites pour les obtenir. Vous dansez, vous avez dansé, et vous continuerez de danser la vile pantomime' (p.181/128). This utterance follows Moi's claims that it would be better to live as a hermit like Diogenes the Cynic (412-323 B.C.), referred to at the beginning of the conversation (p.80/49) and re-introduced here as a concluding ornament.

We must not be misled by the term 'Cynic' which in this context is the name of a school of philosophers who believed that the only true good is virtue. It alone brings happiness, and it consists in avoiding evil and desiring nothing. However, as Moi indicates, the hermit did not go short of sexual partners, and, if need be, he could always resort to masturbation, a practice which Diderot had defended in *Suite de l'Entretien avec D'Alembert*,[3] and which Moi here considers preferable to the indignities and humiliations of the dance of dependency. Moi's argument — an assertion that the quality of life is not exclusively linked to money, the rat-race and luxury, and that Lui's parasitism leads to futile endlessness — is potentially a good one. It seems, however, in contrast to Lui's lengthier statements and colourful presentation to be understated, and the association with onanism looks like a deliberate attempt on Diderot's part to show Moi's argument in a drab and distasteful way. Other cases of this effect are easily found, and we are driven to ask 'Why does Diderot frequently minimise the impact of Moi's points?' A look at the discussion of morality in the earlier part of the book might help us to decide.

The part in question (pp.110-19/72-80) begins and ends with allusions to remorse, considered by several *philosophes* of the

[3] Diderot, *Œuvres philosophiques*, textes établis avec introductions, bibliographies et notes, par Paul Vernière, Classiques Garnier, 1956, pp.372-85; translated by Tancock, *7*, pp.225-33.

time (Madame du Châtelet, La Mettrie, Voltaire, for example)[4] to be a key issue in determining whether a universal moral sense was inborn in all humans, or whether morality was relative, induced by local custom and conditioning. Lui's assertion, that in his activities, remorse is not called for, leads to a discussion upon happiness: is it to be found only in material power and acquisitions (i.e. through money), or is there an innate moral sense, a set of values which impels the individual towards concern for others, truth and virtue, and which must be satisfied if he is to be truly happy?

Moi maintains the latter position, and his first line of defence might be termed 'Civic Virtues': anti-social actions lead to remorse, and the wrong-doer is tormented by 'la voix de la conscience et de l'honneur'; as Moi, through his irony, points out, Lui *ought* to be living 'd'une manière bien honorable pour l'espèce humaine, bien utile à nos concitoyens, bien glorieuse pour vous'. The *philosophes* often put forward such values as the attitudes of the rational man, and readily linked their concepts to the Stoic moralists of Ancient Greece and Rome (e.g. Cato, pp.111-12/74). The precepts included austerity and simplicity of life style, loyalty to one's nation ('la patrie'), and an awareness of the responsibilities of rank or public office, and of the privilege of serving one's fellow citizens: 'un état dans la société'.

Lui dismisses as 'Vanité' these suggested values, and Moi turns next to what we might group as 'Domestic Virtues' (pp.113-15/75-76), principles which Diderot associated with 'états, conditions, relations' in his theories of a socially realistic theatre: bringing up one's children to have healthy moral and financial values, and to avoid vice, social disgrace or ruin; ensuring the honourable conduct of one's wife, one's servants, and one's business affairs. To which Lui replies by counselling

---

[4] For discussions of possible reactions to La Mettrie's amoralism and denial of innate remorse, by Voltaire in *Poème sur la loi naturelle*, 1752, and Diderot in *Le Neveu de Rameau*, see La Mettrie's *L'Homme machine*, critical edition by A. Vartanian, Princeton University Press, 1960, pp.52-54, and *Discours sur le bonheur*, critical edition by J. Falvey, *Studies on Voltaire*, CXXXIV, 1975, pp.92-96, which also studies the close involvement with La Mettrie of Palissot and possibly of Madame Du Châtelet (pp.41-45).

indifference: wife, family and servants should be allowed to do as they please. He makes an exception only for business and money: there he agrees one must 's'y prendre de loin': pay careful attention and plan ahead (compare Lui's plans for his wife, p.182/129).

Finally, Moi produces an eloquent appeal to 'Sentimental Virtue': warm-heartedness and humanity (pp.115-16/76-77). The essence of this kind of morality is that it is personal, a favour done by one individual to another for whom he feels compassion. It could be an act of charity to a stranger, whose plight commands pity (e.g. Voltaire's aid to the persecuted Calas family), or a special kindness in excess of normal duty, towards one's family or close friends, as in the case described by Moi. The motives of such acts were held to be not (primarily) rational, but emotional, affectionate and spontaneous. It was usual to betoken such altruism, or 'sensibilité', by the shedding of tears ('C'est les larmes aux yeux qu'il m'en parlait...') of compassion, by the benefactor, of gratitude by the recipient, and of appreciation by all (including by-standers) of the facts (a) that the human heart was good; (b) that their own goodness as individuals was demonstrated by their ability to be deeply moved by witnessing acts of virtue; and (c) that they could feel in unity and harmony with the rest of mankind, a sense of maudlin solidarity.

In reply to these three forms of moral aspiration in man, Lui has three objections. Firstly, Moi is wrong, he claims, to suppose that these impulsions are common to all men, and that '...il faudrait être d'honnêtes gens pour être heureux', or that one must avoid parasitism, 'se faire une ressource indépendente de la servitude'. According to Lui's observations of life, Moi's moral principles represent 'une espèce de félicité' which is seldom met with, while on the other hand 'une infinité de gens sont heureux sans être honnêtes' (pp.112/74, 115/77-79). Secondly, in his own case, vices come naturally to him, and happiness depends on cultivating them. To try to be virtuous would be to go against his character, and simply make him miserable, while to pretend to find happiness in virtue would be hypocritical, and the reverse of 'honnête'. Finally, Lui refers to 'les mœurs de ma nation': virtue, far from being the rule, is out of fashion, so even genuinely virtuous people, though possibly admired, are certainly not welcome, because their principles make them unsociable, and critical of others. They are also embarrassing, because services to others, far from creating gratitude, produce an unpleasant sense of obligation. Nor is it uncommon for virtuous people to become warped by excess of self-control, and unconsciously hypocritical (pp.112-13/74-75, 117-19/78-79).

Both sides of the argument in this part of the book are cogently and eloquently represented, though Lui's case, with its emphasis on the diversity of individual temperaments, values, and attitudes to virtue, seems more discerning and thus more persuasive. Moreover, Diderot has given Lui the last long statement, so that he is the one whose final words remain with the reader after the subject changes. The summing up of his position, with the forceful 'quelques visionnaires comme vous...' also suggests that Diderot intended Lui's arguments to linger in the mind as the stronger, while Moi, and other *philosophes* should appear, here as elsewhere, as unworldly, abstract 'esprits romanesques'.

In gathering together these several threads of the discussion of morality, we may ask the question 'Can we discern any recommendation to the reader, by Diderot the writer?' Let us look first at the reasons for thinking that Diderot intends us to agree with Moi.

On the face of it, by calling one character 'Moi' Diderot is claiming to identify with that character, and we could argue that any ridicule of Moi (e.g. his appearance, mannerisms, reactions such as becoming shocked or heated at Lui's depravity) must be fairly harmless, and made by Diderot in a spirit of lighthearted frankness. Another reason might be that, although Lui is more logical and persuasive, he presents an immoral nihilistic view which, Diderot might believe, would be patently unacceptable to any reader, on intuitive grounds. We might also argue that this view matches Diderot's satirical processes: Lui and his like (i.e. Palissot, Bertin and Bouret) though powerful and specious, are enemies of society and should be rejected by right-thinking readers. And we could add that the belief put forward by Moi, that each person has an inborn moral conscience, which prompts them towards any or all of the described virtues (civic, domestic or sentimental) and produces remorse in the case of misdemeanours, is in line with views on morality expressed by Diderot in his other writings.

There are, however, difficulties with this interpretation. For one thing, the presentation and techniques used by Diderot favour Lui: his arguments are expounded wittily and at length, they are plentifully illustrated with anecdote, and are humorous, colourful, animated. Moi's arguments are, on the other hand, for the most part tersely stated, with little embellishment. What is more, Diderot has put some dangerously powerful counter-arguments into Lui's mouth, arguments which Moi never answers, so we cannot suppose that Diderot meant to defuse them. One such attack is Lui's claim that individuals vary, and that while some have an inborn impulsion towards virtue, others are impelled towards vice; another is that Moi is taking an abstract, ivory tower view of life in contending that only the *philosophes* are good and independent while the rest of the world is decadent. We can hardly dismiss such arguments as inconsequential playfulness on Diderot's part, for not only are they sound in themselves, but they also hit at vulnerable points in the *philosophes*' position. Their claim that a lay morality existed in all men, and made religion dispensable, was opposed by those who (like Palissot) considered that without the Church's doctrine of eternal retribution, and its authority over conscience and morality, society would fall apart in lawlessness, and who held that the *philosophes* were unworldly intellectuals, blind to the danger of their ideas, and rather like the semi-detached Diogenes of the closing pages.

So it would seem that, if we argue that Moi represents Diderot's views, we must accept also that he has, apparently deliberately, kicked the ball into his own goal. Let us therefore consider the possibility that Diderot intends us to agree with Lui. Reasons to support this would be that Lui's analyses of his own motives, and of those of the society in which he moves, are presented as honest (we are repeatedly told that he is not a hypo-

moi conceals many things

crite and not concealing anything from Moi); his arguments are resourceful and highly intelligent; and he is a captivating and gifted personality. It is true that his amoralism runs counter to everything Diderot upheld elsewhere, but since he kept the manuscript of *Le Neveu de Rameau* secret, it could well be that he was thinking through his private thoughts to their conclusion, one which was so corrosive and disruptive that he intended never to publish it.

What are the difficulties in accepting this interpretation? Much could be made of the critical portrayal of Lui as lacking in 'dignité', 'conséquence', persistence or moral fibre. But if we look for Diderot's technical guidance, it is to be noted that Lui's misdemeanours become progressively more despicable as the tale draws to its close. The third of the possible endings we have examined represents the close of intellectual play, but Diderot's control over our reactions continues. What follows is an end-piece, a kind of coda; in it, Lui's genius for mime, for parasitism, his devotion to money and his comicality are neatly brought together in a way which reveals a new and shocking depth to his depravity. He praises the beauty and gifts of his exquisite wife, now deceased, and her courage in accepting an unpleasant way of life for love of him. To make his point he describes her anatomy, and gives an erotic mime of her walk and manner, disclosing his plans to make his fortune by hiring her out as a prostitute. The passage ends with him collapsing in tears at the loss of her — because his plans have come to nothing.

It would seem that through this story, which has in some measure been prepared by the emphasis on the need for concern about the behaviour of one's wife (pp.113-14/75) and through the tale of the Jew and *le grison* (pp.174-75/123-24), Diderot has tried to make it more difficult for the reader to condone Lui's lack of responsibility and moral principle. A third possible interpretation might therefore be that he does not intend us to agree either with Moi or with Lui, or to perceive any coherent indication from himself as to what we should believe. He intends only to exemplify the difficulties of the question of morality, personal and social, and to leave the dialogue going on unresolved in the reader's mind.

Towards/ copralalia

MATERIALISM v. LIBERTINAGE

NO LOST, ONLY MATERIAL GAIN

If we take this view, Diderot's purposes in under-playing the force of Moi's arguments and personality can be understood as a regulating technique by which he constantly controls and balances the effect on the reader. Having set up the tension between the two speakers, and given Lui a more explicit presentation, because his argument and life-style are unusual, Diderot has carefully preserved the balance of persuasiveness through the three possible endings, or impasses, which tend to present Lui's side more attractively, and the final anecdote about his wife and his abandonment of all values except acquisitiveness, which restores the fine equilibrium by reminding us of the unsavoury side of Lui.

The close combination of Diderot's artistry and argument, apparent particularly in the final discussion of morality, is well exemplified in this closing image of Lui's wife, enticing followers and turning on them, recalling the opening image of the *catins* in the Palais Royal gardens. The close of the dialogue, with Lui off to the Opera, reminds us of another ambiguous dimension in the problematic values he represents: is he escaping from his grief by plunging back into the shiny but empty world of money-dominated entertainment, or is he, like the (then) well-known music-devotee, Abbé de Causaye, ascending into a realm of elevated beauty, harmony and purity, the world he had conjured up for Moi in his great mime, and one in which his moral ugliness, like that of the genius, is transcended by his artistic sensitivity and exaltation?

# Conclusion

We have now looked closely at each of the major component parts of *Le Neveu de Rameau*, and the time has come to evaluate the work as a whole. We may begin by asking 'How well do the parts fit together?'

A measure of coherence is brought to the work by the discussion of genius, in which three possible forms of excellence in unconventional fields are suggested for Lui. An odd evaluative problem is presented by one of these, namely Lui's excellence in musical matters. It seems clear, as already noted in the conclusion to the chapter on music, that Diderot means us to see Lui as a genuinely gifted musician, a fully trained instrumentalist, specialising in harpsichord and possibly violin, and a profound and revelatory seer. However, it has for a long time been believed that Diderot himself was not very competent in musical matters, and although some recent studies have partially rehabilitated him in this respect,[5] it seems nevertheless that despite his early training in singing, possibly as a chorister, and a passionate love of music, he was probably ungifted, and remained largely untutored.

His labours on the *Encyclopédie* left no time for diversions for an interval of seven years, and after a couple of pamphlets written in 1753 during the *Guerre des bouffons* (*Au petit prophète* and *Les trois chapitres*), it was not until 1760 that he resumed contact with the world of music and musicians. He first looked closely into instrument playing, it seems, towards 1771, when with his quick and efficient grasp, cultivated through writing 'fill-in' articles for the *Encyclopédie* when no specialist editor could be found, he wrote up, after attending at his

[5] e.g. Jean-Michel Bardez, *Diderot et la musique. Valeur de la contribution d'un mélomane*. Champion, Bibl. de littérature comparée, 1975; Diderot, *Œuvres complètes*, tome XIX, *Musique*, édition critique et annotée, par J. Mayer et P. Citron, avec les soins de J. Varloot, Hermann, 1983. See especially pages ix-xxii: 'Diderot et la musique'.

daughter's music-lessons, a competent manual, *Leçons de clavecin et principes d'harmonie* by Bemetzreider, the harpsichord teacher. It will be remembered that the section on music showed signs of being written in 1761 and never subsequently updated. It is thus possible that Lui might appear, to readers well versed in musical matters, to be under-informed, and something of a tyro or even a charlatan in music.

We are therefore left to ask ourselves 'Has Diderot succeeded in inducing in the reader at least the *illusion* that Lui is a person of exceptional musical gifts, one from whom unique insights into the realities of the art can be gained?' Or ought we instead to demand that his utterances should be, in fact as well as in fiction, totally satisfying to the expert in musicology, and authentic contributions to the history and theory of the art? In the individual's conclusion on these questions, much will inevitably depend on whether he accepts and judges *Le Neveu de Rameau* as a work of creative fiction, or as a statement by Diderot made in encyclopaedic terms.

A second discussion of genius, 'le sublime en mal', ends in a position which Diderot has deliberately made unsatisfying. In the first place, 'le mal' does not seem a very accurate term for the crimes being measured and compared: they turn out to be not the cosmic evil-doing of Milton's Lucifer, nor mass-murders on the epic scale (not unknown in Diderot's times), nor even tales of romanticised criminals with a noble streak (e.g. Prévost's Des Grieux, or later, Balzac's Vautrin). They are instead 'evil' on the scale of petty and covert treachery, sharp practice and greed, which conflict less with the law than with the sense of human decency and decorum.

In the second place, Bouret's prize-winning crime, when judged on the evidence and argument supplied in the text, is a non-starter, even in terms of 'mean-mindedness'. So we must conclude that the theme of 'genius in evil' has been introduced mainly for satirical purposes, and has been rapidly abandoned by Diderot as a topic for serious exploration in its own right, and that in this area of the argument, only generalised inferences are being advanced, namely that productions of genius need not necessarily be associated with good intentions, nor need they be recognisable as works of genius, for in the eyes of contemporaries they may seem as trivial as the alienation of the affections of a dog.

Such broad considerations serve as framework to the third distinction, claimed by Lui, genius in parasitism. At first this also might be thought of as a frivolous idea, brought in mainly for the satire, but within the context of the book, 'parasitism' in some form, even if only emotional dependency on another, is a basic ingredient of human existence, in the dance of life, 'le grand branle de la terre'. Thus to be able to innovate in this sphere, to establish it as an artistic discipline, might be seen as the most important field for the manifestation of human genius and progress.

Here again we meet a question which can only be resolved by each reader for himself. Is Diderot regarding parasitism as invariably a bad thing, and re-defining evil, not as a spectacular confrontation with God or the law, but as a tawdry, drab, heartless exploitation of everyone and everything for their profitability? Or is he on the other hand saying that parasitism is neither good nor bad, that people or acts which society might call 'evil', are simply part of Nature, a struggle for survival in an amoral, biological universe?

The strangeness resulting from considering these themes together intensifies if we turn to the section on music. For in the history of this art, genius and evolutionary progress take the form of revolt, and renewal of contact with the fundamental sources of inspiration. In this, Lui, Moi and presumably Diderot seem united on the side of the revolutionists, the new wave of innovators with their 'grass roots' revitalisation. Similarly, Moi accepts Lui's innovation in miming as a valid musical achievement and experience. The oddness lies in that, in the context, the equivalents of the inspirational musical innovator, the genius, in the world of parasitism, are not the *Encyclopédistes*, but Lui, Bouret, Palissot and other adroit operators, who are thus aligned, not with the monolithic establishment, as we might have expected from Diderot, but with the progressive, fertile anarchists.

When we consider these sections on genius and music in con-

junction with the section on satire, the oddness is even more
apparent. Lui, in his skilfully vicious capacity, represents the
*mores* of Diderot's enemies, and exposes them from the inside.
Within the section of the book devoted to satire, the irony
works, and criticism and mockery are successfully achieved. But
elsewhere in the book, the discussions on genius and the
development of music by cyclical movements have favoured
those who defy the establishment, convention, and even (in the
justification of evil in geniuses, like Socrates) accepted ideas of
human decency. And if we turn to the debate on morality in the
hope of a unifying coherence, we are likely to be disappointed.

It is true that the final symbol of the dance cleverly
recapitulates in terms of images the satire of Bouret and friends.
But if Diderot had wished to complete this satirical structure, he
would have had to present the discussion of morality, at least in
these closing stages, as being manifestly in support of Moi's
rectitude and altruism. Instead, he leaves the moral question
balanced, and in some ways, it seems (especially if we were to
limit our reading of Diderot to *Le Neveu de Rameau* alone) as if
he is more in favour of Lui's pessimistic but creative lawlessness
as an interpretation of man's destiny, than of Moi's isolationist
and sterile misanthropy. Such uncertainty and ambiguity, while
excellent in opening up new dimensions in the novel and in the
ruminations of the reader, is of course no good for satire, for it
is likely to confuse the public. In this instance, the vigour of the
satire is severely reduced by the accompanying discussion of
morality, which suggests that 'tout comprendre c'est tout par-
donner', and hence that there is nothing wrong with the motives
of anyone, including Diderot's enemies.

So it seems that when we look at the parts of this book
separately, they make reasonable sense, but when we consider
them in relation to one another, they clash in a bewildering
manner. It is a final oddness that while one might expect these
incongruities and incoherences to spoil the book, in practice they
do not seem to. To explain this, we are brought back to the well
used but very helpful simile of the hanging mobile decoration, in
which each part is a linked but separable component, making
differing senses in differing conjunctions, and initiating further

dialogues in the reader's mind.

Having surveyed the major themes of the work, let us now turn to the subsidiary themes. In this respect the work is very rich, for these themes are too numerous to be exhaustively noticed or dealt with here. Some we have looked at (e.g. the ideas on education, and on *métiers*), but others can be discerned and developed, particularly if we allow our imaginations to respond to the stimuli of the text. Some of these minor themes are philosophical ideas in themselves. To pick more or less at random one of a number of good examples of a well worked-out idea-theme, an article by Beatrice Fink (*13*) takes 'eating', the prime concern of the parasite at all biological levels, and shows how universally it recurs and how profoundly it ties in with the interpretation of the work.

Or again, a whole group of themes is to be found in the suggestion of theories of economics, both micro- and macro-, in Diderot's indications of the power of money. An attack on capitalism and its evils could easily be read into the text; or a defence of laisser-faire commercial liberalism; or a discussion of the quality of life in an affluent urban society. The references to dwelling places and other habitats (e.g. cafés, public gardens), to animals, to body-language, to prostitution, to gamesmanship, and to life-skills of other kinds, would all provide, or have already provided, fruitful lines of exploration.

Other themes, less related to substance, are more closely connected with presentational techniques, to manner, or to decorative embellishment. Examples can be seen in the recurrence of references to *la masque*, *les pagodes*, and — expectedly — to chess, both in terms of the pieces (king, queen, bishop, courtiers, pawns etc.) and of the moves: e.g. the three possible endings, which we have discussed as 'impasses', might alternatively have been thought of as attempts at check and mate. Several studies exist on the analogies with chess: less noticed are the possible analogies with that most pervasive of eighteenth-century mythologies and thinking tokens, the Tarot cards: see for example Le Fou, the jester, ever changing, discovering the delights and pitfalls of the world, ever innocent because irresponsible. We could find comparisons with Lui (pp.117/78, 133-34/91-92), and we could find allusions to some of the other major arcana cards, e.g. the Wheel of Fortune (p.176/124-25), the lamp-bearing Hermit (cf. Diogène, pp.180-81/127-28), L'Etoile (cf. l'astre, p.170/119) and the Dance of the World (pp.178-79/125-27); and of the four suits of cards, Coins at least are amply indicated.

There are also a number of recurrent thematic motifs for which there seems, in many cases, to be no obvious explanation, although they appear to be deliberate inclusions on Diderot's part. Why, for example, is he so critical of Clairon and her acting at almost every mention?[6] It was Clairon alone, in all the Comédie Française troupe, who stood out against the staging of *Les Philosophes* and Diderot owed her a debt of gratitude. Why are there so many references to time and its running out (especially pp.97-110/62-72), rather too persistent and diversified to be fully explained as part of the 'time is money' theme? And why does Diderot from time to time repeat, almost in the same words, passages of the text (e.g. pp.111-12/74; cf. pp.130/88, 142-43/98-99)? Sometimes the repetition can be explained as a deliberate cross-reference, a link with the same idea, being picked up for further treatment; but other instances look like accidental repetition, possibly caused by re-working the text. As in the case of the major themes, we can find only a limited possibility of explaining and integrating these images, symbols and devices.

To draw together and sum up these various evaluative comments, the book may be adversely criticised for its subjectivity, the cause of many incoherences and enigmas which any author might reasonably be expected to have clarified. The fact that Diderot seems not to have intended to publish the text explains, but does not reduce, these defects. Yet whatever gravity the individual reader places upon them, they have had the effect of affording scope for both scholars and non-specialists to involve themselves intimately with the work. Furthermore, the inclusion of the satire, and the reflections of

---

[6] The references to Clairon on pages 34/48, and 59/69, are unfavourable; those on pages 78-80/85-87, though declared in a general way to be ironic, present many unfavourable details.

the world of contemporary music, despite their rough-edged interfaces, inject life, bustle and humour into the writing. We can thus notice that, considered as a novel, *Le Neveu de Rameau* positively benefits by the incongruities and gaps. To an even greater extent, it benefits from the fact that the debate on morality, behaviour and the motivating forces of society is left unresolved, for it thus serves as a statement of man's position when confronting the ambivalent nature of morality itself, a dilemma which Diderot, through Lui, deliberately leaves with the reader: 'Rira bien qui rira le dernier'.

It is the combination of a number of inconclusive, unresolved elements which creates the vibrant background lighting for the dialogue of ideas, around which the other parts of the mobile revolve, and in particular for the central portrait of Lui, brought to life and caught unforgettably in all his barely credible animation. By an enlivening paradox, we are left feeling that, amid the abundance of obscurities, enigmas and loose ends, the one thing that has been revealed totally, honestly and unhypo- critically is the character and energy of Lui, this instructive specimen, exploiter and victim of cultural mankind.

# Select Bibliography

Unless otherwise stated, the place of publication of items in French is Paris. Numbers *1* and *2* below are the editions referred to here.

## A. EDITIONS

1. *Le Neveu de Rameau, Le Rêve de d'Alembert*, introductions, notes et annexes de Roland Desné et de Jean Varloot, Editions Sociales, Coll. Essentiel, 1984. Desné's introduction and footnotes, basically those of 1972 (see *16* below), are updated and amplified. The text is revised in the light of J. Chouillet's edition (see *6* below). Other valuable features are the 'index des noms cités', 'glossaire', and italicisation of the non-dialogue passages.

2. *Le Neveu de Rameau*, introduction, notes, chronologie, dossier, bibliographie par Jean-Claude Bonnet, Flammarion, Collection 'GF', 1983. Introduction and dossier are substantial; replaces *4* below in this collection.

3. *Le Neveu de Rameau*, édition critique avec notes et lexique par Jean Fabre, Genève/Lille, Droz, Coll. Textes Littéraires Français, 1950. Introduction (pp.vii-xcv) is particularly important; notes are remarkably full. I have drawn heavily on this source for details, information and interpretation, but to avoid excess of notes have indicated the debt only where it seemed particularly pertinent to do so.

4. *Le Neveu de Rameau*, chronologie et préface par Antoine Adam, Flammarion, Collection 'GF', 1967. Preface is concise, vigorous, rather contentious. Text attractively printed. But see *2* above.

5. *Le Neveu de Rameau, Satires, Contes et Entretiens*, édition établie et commentée par Jacques et Anne-Marie Chouillet, Le Livre de Poche, 1984. Reliable text, interesting comments; and accompanying texts not otherwise easily accessible.

6. *Le Neveu de Rameau; satire seconde*, texte présenté et commenté par Jacques Chouillet, illustrations de Michel Otthoffer, Imprimerie Nationale, Coll. Lettres Françaises, 1982. Well established text, notes are especially good for section on music. Luxuriously produced.

7. *Rameau's Nephew and D'Alembert's Dream*, translated with introductions by Leonard Tancock, Harmondsworth, Penguin Books, 1966. Accurate, reliable, with informative introduction and endnotes.

8. *Rameaus Neffe: ein Dialog von Diderot*, aus dem Manuskript übersetzt und mit Anmerkungen begleitet von Goethe, Leipzig: G.J. Goschen, 1805.

9. *Le Neveu de Rameau*, précédé d'une étude de Goethe sur Diderot, suivi de l'analyse de *La Fin du monde* et du *Neveu de Rameau* de M. Jules Janin, Librairie de la Bibliothèque Nationale, 1879.

10. *Le Neveu de Rameau et autres dialogues philosophiques*, préface de Jean Varloot, Gallimard, Coll. Folio, 1972. Preface mainly concerned with Diderot 'homme du dialogue'.

## B. SAMPLE SELECTION OF CRITICAL COMMENT, INTERPRETATION, AND BACKGROUND STUDIES

11. Charles Palissot de Montenoi, *Les Philosophes*, édition critique avec introduction et notes par T.J. Barling, Exeter, University of Exeter, Coll. Textes littéraires, 1975.

12. Otis Fellows, 'The theme of genius in Diderot's *Le Neveu de Rameau*', *Diderot Studies*, II (1952), pp.168-99.

13. Beatrice Fink, 'A parasitic reading of Diderot's *Le Neveu de Rameau*', *Forum*, XVI, 2 (1981), pp.19-25.

14. Anthony Strugnell, 'Les fonctions textuelles du moi dans deux dialogues philosophiques de Diderot', *Studies on Voltaire*, CCVIII (1982), pp.175-81. Though not on *Le Neveu de Rameau*, is interesting by way of comparison.

15. Yoishi Sumi, *'Le Neveu de Rameau': caprices et logiques du jeu*, Tokyo, Tosho, 1975.

16. Two prefaces, by Jean Varloot (pp.5-18) and by Maurice Roelens (pp.19-36), are included in the 1972 edition of *Le Neveu de Rameau*, introductions et commentaires de Roland Desné, Editions Sociales, Coll. Classiques du peuple. In the new 1984 Editions Sociales text (see *1* on the list of editions above) these two essays do not appear.

17. Morris Wachs, 'The identity of the renégat d'Avignon', *Studies on Voltaire*, XC (1972), pp.1747-56.

## C. FURTHER BIBLIOGRAPHY

More complete bibliographies will be found in: Chouillet, *6* above, who also lists sixteen stage versions; Sumi, *15* above; Bonnet, *2* above, and Fabre, *3* above. Up-to-date bibliographical essays or guidance are given in: Peter France, *Diderot*, Oxford/New York, OUP, Past Masters series, 1983; F. Spear, *Bibliographie de Diderot, répertoire analytique international*, Geneva, Droz, 1980; A.-M. and J. Chouillet, 'Etat actuel des recherches sur Diderot', *Dix-huitième siècle*, XII (1980), pp.443-70.

# CRITICAL GUIDES TO FRENCH TEXTS

*edited by*

Roger Little, Wolfgang van Emden, David Williams